FAMILY LAW BASICS

Author: Cheryl Bowman

Publisher: CleverQuill Publishing

DISCLAIMER

This publication provides accurate and authoritative information regarding the subject matter covered. Neither the author nor the publisher is engaged in rendering legal, investment, accounting, or other professional services. While the author has used their best efforts in preparing this book, they make no representations or warranties with respect to the accuracy or completeness of the contents of this book and specifically disclaim any implied warranties of merchantability or fitness for a particular purpose. No warranty may be created or extended by sales representatives or written sales materials. The information contained herein may not be suitable for your situation. You should consult with a professional when appropriate. The author shall not be liable for any loss of profit or any other commercial damages, including but not limited to special, incidental, consequential, personal, or other damages.

DEDICATION

For Fred, who taught me everything I know about Florida family law—and then some.

A Note from the Author

"Family Law Basics" replaces "Florida Family Law Basics." I am expanding this to include information for all states. I am also incorporating the second book, "Florida Family Law Basics: Discovery," into this book rather than creating two separate books.

"FAMILY LAW BASICS" IS NOT LEGAL ADVICE AND IS NOT WRITTEN BY AN ATTORNEY.

ACKNOWLEDGEMENTS

A special thank you to Michelle Romano, MSW, LICSW, for her invaluable assistance in editing this book. Michelle's keen eye for detail, expertise in language, and unwavering commitment to clarity greatly enhanced the quality of this work.

Her thoughtful suggestions and meticulous attention to spelling, grammar, and overall readability ensured that the final manuscript communicates its ideas with precision and accessibility. I am deeply grateful for her time, professionalism, and support throughout this process.

TABLE OF CONTENTS

INTRODUCTION

Purpose and Scope

I wrote "Florida Family Law Basics" and "Florida Family Law Basics: Discovery" as concise guides for individuals navigating a Florida divorce. I found that people were often overwhelmed by the divorce process, regardless of how much an attorney explained it. There is a lot of information to take in at one time, and it is very easy to forget what the attorney explained during a short family law consultation.

Although people want to divorce for various reasons, it is often an emotionally trying time. Additionally, both parties face financial uncertainty, as they are aware that they will have to divide assets and create a time-sharing schedule.

Those who own businesses may face even more turmoil, wondering how property division will impact the company and whether they will have to allow a spouse to continue working in the business.

While **this book is not intended to provide legal advice,** it can help guide you through the divorce process and offer a better understanding of what may happen. Use it in conjunction with your attorney's advice to make the divorce process smoother.

Many people have downloaded the book since I originally published the first edition of each book in 2011. Since then, laws have changed, and more people want to understand the process better and hopefully save a little money by preparing for divorce prior to meeting with an attorney.

This new edition combines Family Law Basics and Family Law Discovery and encompasses family law for all states instead of only Florida. It will contain general information about the process that you can use regardless of which state you are in.

I hope you find "Family Law Basics" helpful and informational.

Overview of Family Law and Its Importance

Family law governs the rights, responsibilities and relationships within families. It encompasses issues such as marriage, divorce, property division, child custody, child support, spousal support (alimony), adoption and domestic violence. This book addresses all issues except for adoption.

The scope of family law encompasses the formation of a family relationship—marriage—to its dissolution, including legal separation and custody arrangements. At its core, family law serves to protect the interests of family members, especially children. It provides a legal framework to resolve disputes and allocate financial responsibilities fairly. It also provides the framework to protect a child's welfare and ensure children have the support and stability required for healthy development.

How to Use This Book

Family Law Basics is a practical, accessible guide for anyone seeking to understand the fundamentals of family law. Whether you are facing a family law issue, supporting a loved one or simply want to learn more about this area of law, this book will help you navigate the process with confidence and clarity.

You do not need to read every chapter, though doing so will give you the whole picture. Some readers may know some of the basics, while others, especially those who have never filed a lawsuit or been sued, may need to read the very basics.

Refer to the endnotes for sources, forms or additional instructions where applicable.

Navigating the Chapters

Each chapter of this book focuses on a specific aspect of family law, such as divorce, property division, child custody and more. Key features include clear explanations, practical tips, state variations and resources.

Limitations

THIS BOOK IS INTENDED AS A GENERAL GUIDE AND DOES NOT REPLACE PERSONALIZED LEGAL ADVICE FROM A QUALIFIED ATTORNEY. FAMILY LAW CAN BE COMPLEX AND FACT-SPECIFIC, AND LAWS CHANGE OVER TIME.

ALWAYS CONSULT A LEGAL PROFESSIONAL FOR ADVICE ABOUT YOUR PARTICULAR CIRCUMSTANCES.

I AM NOT A LAWYER AND CANNOT GIVE LEGAL ADVICE. ALWAYS OBTAIN LEGAL ADVICE FROM AN EXPERIENCED ATTORNEY. THIS BOOK IS ONLY A GUIDE TO HELP YOU UNDERSTAND YOUR ATTORNEY'S INSTRUCTIONS.

Family Law Basics is here to empower you with knowledge, reduce uncertainty and help you make informed decisions during some of life's most challenging moments.

Cheryl Bowman

FAMILY LAW BASICS
PART 1: DIVORCE

CHAPTER 1: UNDERSTANDING DIVORCE

When you can no longer live together, it may be time to file for divorce. This step in your life can bring about a lot of uncertainty, especially if you have children, high assets or a business. All states offer some form of uncontested divorce, and all states provide default divorce. Regardless of which type of divorce you file or end up with, they all serve the purpose of dividing assets, determining child custody and support, and determining spousal support (alimony).

Divorce ends a marriage—think of it as ending a contract. When you and your spouse cannot agree on the factors of divorce, the court will make those decisions for you. It is a significant legal and personal event that affects the spouses involved, as well as children, extended family and social circles.

Divorce is the legal dissolution of a marriage by a court. Once the court finalizes the divorce, both parties can remarry, as they are no longer legally bound as spouses. However, some states enter a judgment *nisi*, which means the divorce is not absolute until a specific period of time ***after*** the entry of the judgment *nisi*.

During divorce proceedings, the court resolves several issues, including property division, child custody, child support and spousal support.

Common Reasons for Divorce

Each person's situation is unique; however, research and court records reveal several recurring reasons people decide to end their marriages:

- **Lack of Commitment**: One or both spouses are no longer committed to the relationship, and the marriage breaks down.
- **Constant Conflict**: Unresolved conflicts and persistent arguing create an unhealthy environment, making one or both spouses uncomfortable. The constant bickering can also affect your children.
- **Infidelity**: One or both spouses have an extramarital affair, which erodes trust and intimacy. Reconciliation without trust is very difficult.
- **Domestic Violence**: Abuse can be physical, emotional and/or financial. Any type of abuse is a serious reason for divorce. Always prioritize your safety and that of your children.
- **Communication Issues**: Poor communication often prevents couples from resolving issues, even those that most people otherwise resolve easily, making for an unhealthy relationship.
- **Growing Apart**: When you have a difference in interests, life goals and values, it can lead to incompatibility.
- **External Family Pressures**: Interference and/or pressure from extended family members often contribute to marital discord.
- **Parenting Differences**: Disagreements about how you raise your children, including educational, religious and medical decisions, can put undue strain on a marriage.

The Divorce Process

Each state has its own divorce laws and procedures. However, most follow a similar sequence of steps, some of which we will address in full in subsequent chapters. These steps include:

- Prepare to file for divorce or legal separation by gathering financial and other documents required for the divorce process.
- Retain a family law attorney.
- Turn in all documents required for mandatory disclosure.
- File the Petition for Dissolution of Marriage.
- Serve the Petition on your spouse.

- Wait for your spouse's response.

- If your spouse files a counter-petition, file an answer to the counter-petition.

- If you are not using an attorney, forward a **_copy_** of your disclosure to your spouse.

- File a notice of compliance with mandatory disclosure with the court ('Mandatory disclosure' may be referred to in other terms by some states).

- File any motions for temporary requests for support, custody or the use of property during the pendency of divorce.

- Negotiate or attend mediation. Some counties in various states may require mediation.

- Go to trial if you cannot settle your differences.

- Review the Final Judgment of Dissolution of Marriage (Divorce Decree in some states) after the court executes and signs it.

Emotional and Practical Considerations

Not only is divorce a legal process, but it is also an emotional one. It is often stressful and overwhelming, especially when you have children or significant financial or property issues.

Consulting with a family law attorney and seeking emotional support can help you navigate the process more effectively. Understanding the basics of family law and the procedure can also help you make more informed decisions and have more confidence and clarity throughout the entire process.

CHAPTER 2: TYPES OF DIVORCE

Each state has its own divorce laws, but most states offer contested and uncontested divorces. Some may refer to an uncontested divorce by other names. The types of divorce include:

- No-fault
- Fault-based
- Uncontested
- Contested
- Simplified (summary)
- Default
- Pro Se
- Covenant marriage
- Divorce from bed and board

No-Fault Divorce

A no-fault divorce is available in all states. In 16 states plus Washington, D.C., no-fault divorce is the only option.

In a no-fault divorce, the spouses do not have to prove wrongdoing by the other party. The common grounds, depending on your state, include irreconcilable differences or irretrievable breakdown of the marriage.

The states with no-fault-only divorce include:

California	Colorado	Florida	Hawaii	Illinois
Iowa	Kentucky	Michigan	Minnesota	Missouri
Montana	Nebraska	Nevada	Oregon	Washington
Wisconsin	Washington, D.C.			

In most states, one spouse can file unilaterally—without permission from the other. However, Mississippi, South Dakota and Tennessee all require mutual consent to file a no-fault divorce.

In some cases, Tennessee allows unilateral divorce. However, to ensure your situation qualifies, speak with a Tennessee family law attorney.

Fault-Based Divorce

In a fault-based divorce, you must be able to prove marital misconduct, such as adultery. Fault-based divorce is still available in some states. Each state's laws outline the grounds under which you can file for divorce. If you allege grounds, you must be able to prove any ground you allege in the divorce petition.

Grounds may include:

- Impotence (some states may require impotence at the time of marriage)
- Polygamy (married to two people at the same time)
- Adultery
- Desertion (some states may require willful or malicious desertion, some states may implement a time period, such as one year, for desertion without reasonable cause)
- Commission of a crime (usually a felony or a crime that makes the guilty party infamous)
- Attempted murder of your spouse
- Pregnant by another man at the time of marriage (without knowledge of the husband)

- Substance abuse

- Cruel and inhuman treatment / domestic violence

- Abandonment

- Irreconcilable differences

- Separation (some states may have a time requirement, such as being legally separated for two years)

Uncontested Divorce

Every state offers uncontested divorce, though they may call it different names, including:

- Divorce with Agreement on All Issues

- Decree Upon Affidavit

- Uncontested Dissolution of Marriage

- Divorce by Stipulation

- Summary Divorce

- Joint Petition for Divorce

- Separation Agreement Divorce

Contested Divorce

You must file a contested divorce and serve your spouse with a divorce petition if you do not agree on at least one factor. For example, you may agree on custody, time-sharing, child support and property division, but not on alimony. You must file a contested divorce.

However, you can also file a Partial Marital Settlement for the factors you agree on. Filing a Partial Marital Settlement Agreement can significantly decrease the time it takes to litigate.

Settlement During Divorce Proceedings

Filing a contested divorce does not mean that you cannot settle during the divorce proceedings. Many couples go to mediation with a disinterested third party who helps them reach a settlement.

Should you reach a full settlement after filing a contested divorce, you do not have a trial. Instead, you attend an uncontested final hearing. Depending on your state's laws, one or both spouses must appear to "prove up" the divorce.

Summary/Simplified Divorce

Some states offer a summary or simplified divorce in addition to an uncontested divorce. This is an expedited process, which is usually short for couples with no kids and limited assets/debts. The requirements vary from state to state. An experienced family law attorney can advise you as to whether your state offers a simplified divorce and what the qualifications are.

Default Divorce

When you file a contested divorce, your spouse must file responsive pleadings within a set number of days as dictated by your state's laws. Standard time frames for filing responsive pleadings include 20 to 45 days.

If your spouse does not respond to your divorce petition, you can schedule a "default hearing for divorce" with the court. If your spouse does not show up for the default hearing, you will receive everything you asked for in your divorce petition.

If your spouse does show up for the default hearing, the court will hear his or her excuse for not filing timely responsive pleadings. In most cases, the court will allow your spouse an additional number of days—often 10 to 15—to file responsive pleadings.

Should your spouse not file responsive pleadings during the additional time, the court usually grants the default divorce.

What Are Responsive Pleadings?

A responsive pleading is one filed in response to a petition, complaint or motion filed with the court. In the case of divorce, the most common responsive pleading is an "Answer to Divorce Petition," often referred to as an "Answer."

However, respondents can file:

- **Motion to Dismiss**: Asks the court to dismiss the divorce petition, motion or complaint. The moving party must provide a valid reason based on state laws to dismiss the case.
- **Motion for Extension of Time**: Asks the court to grant extra time to respond to the petition, complaint or motion. It is common to request a motion for an extension of time when the moving party needs additional time to locate an attorney or the chosen attorney received the pleadings less than a week prior to the answer's due date.

Pro Se Divorce

Filing for a divorce without the guidance of an attorney is a *pro se* divorce. Most states provide forms with instructions on state or county websites.

** Warning: Divorce laws are complex, especially when you have children or high assets. We do not recommend filing a *pro se* divorce if you and your spouse do not agree on all factors, or if you have children and/or a significant number of assets or a business.

Covenant Marriage Divorce

A covenant marriage is available in Louisiana, Arkansas and Arizona. When a couple agrees to a covenant marriage, it is supposed to be for life. To opt for a covenant marriage, the couple must undergo counseling prior to the marriage and sign an affidavit or statement on the marriage license.

The couple must also agree that they must file limited grounds for separation or dissolution of a covenant marriage.

If you have a covenant marriage, including converting a regular marriage into a covenant marriage, you can only file a covenant divorce.

Depending on your state, the requirements to file for a divorce from a covenant marriage include:

- You must prove one of the following grounds:
  - Adultery,

- o Your spouse committed a felony that resulted in imprisonment or a death sentence,
- o Abandonment,
- o Physical or sexual abuse,
- o Substance abuse,
- o Cruel treatment or
- o Living separate and apart, usually for one or two years, depending on your state.
- You must attend marriage counseling to attempt to resolve your issues.
- You must file a Complaint for Divorce stating the specific ground or grounds. You must also provide factual allegations to support the grounds.

As with a regular divorce, you, or your attorney on your behalf, must legally serve your spouse, who shall have a certain amount of time to respond. If your spouse disputes the grounds, the court holds a hearing to determine if you met the requirements for filing a covenant divorce.

Also, if you choose to separate or must separate legally pursuant to state law, the separation period is often longer than in standard divorces.

CHAPTER 3: RESIDENCY REQUIREMENTS

Most states have residency requirements to file for divorce (Appendix I). These rules ensure the state's courts have jurisdiction to hear your case. They also prevent "forum shopping," where a party might look for a state with more favorable divorce laws.

You must be able to provide a state identification card or driver's license with an issue date prior to the date you file your petition. The issue date cannot be after the date you file for divorce, as it must show that you have lived in the state for the required amount of time.

Some states also have specific time frames for living in a county in addition to state requirements. We have included the relevant state statute at the time of publication for your convenience.

State laws often change. If you are filing *pro se*, be sure to conduct thorough research before filing. If you are working with an attorney, check with him or her for updated residency requirements.

Definition of Residency Requirements and Time Frames

A fundamental legal rule throughout the United States for divorce cases is that residency requirements determine whether a state court has jurisdiction (authority) to grant a divorce. Depending on the state, it may require that you are domiciled in the state, while others only require residency. Some states even use the two terms interchangeably.

A "residence" is the place where you currently live, even if temporarily. This is common with servicemembers in the armed forces. You can have multiple residences, for example, a main home and a vacation home. If you spend four months in your vacation home, that is your residence for those four months, while your main home is your residence for the other eight months of the year.

A "domicile" is your permanent home—the place you intend to return to and remain indefinitely. While you can have two or more residences, you can only have one domicile at a time.

Courts generally require that at least one spouse has a genuine, ongoing connection to the state, meaning domicile.

Each state has its own residency requirements. While the requirements can range from no waiting period to a year or more, the most common requirement is six months. Some states also have a second requirement that you must be a resident of the **county** in which you are filing. It is often 30 to 90 days, depending on the state, though some may have requirements outside of that time frame.

Failure to Meet Residency Requirements

If you file for divorce and have not met your state's residency requirements, the court could dismiss your case for lack of jurisdiction. In most cases, you will have to refile once you meet the residency requirements, which means paying another filing fee. If a court does not have jurisdiction, it cannot legally issue a final divorce decree or any other order for child custody, support issues and property distribution.

However, you may be able to file in the state where you have residency, though several issues arise, including paying another filing fee and travel expenses to attend hearings.

If you are filing a fault-based divorce, it could also alert your spouse, giving him or her enough time to dispose of or hide evidence, which could affect your case.

A dismissal can also cause significant delays and additional legal expenses, as the court could void any proceedings or temporary orders it may have issued.

Special Considerations and Exceptions

Many states have special considerations and exceptions for meeting the residency requirement for certain classes of people, including military members, those involved in domestic violence cases and other circumstances.

Miltary Members

Because the military assigns servicemembers to bases that may be out of their home states (domicile), they often receive an exception to the residency requirements, allowing them to file for divorce without meeting the requirements.

In some cases, because the servicemember's assignment lasts longer than the residency requirement and he or she did not file for divorce until after the requirement expired, the court has jurisdiction, even though the servicemember and/or his or her spouse do not plan to remain in the state on a permanent basis.

While courts generally consider the servicemember's domicile, they also allow filing in the state of his or her current assignment. The Servicemembers Civil Relief Act (SCRA) also permits the servicemember to postpone divorce proceedings if military duties affect participation. The court generally grants a 90-day stay in these situations.

Domestic Violence

If a party is in an abusive situation, the court may deem it an emergency and can waive the residency requirement in order to protect the victim and provide access to legal remedies.

Child Custody Cases

The Uniform Child Custody Jurisdiction and Enforcement Act (UCCJEA)[i] governs jurisdiction over children and prioritizes the child's home state. If a child has lived in a state for at least six consecutive months, the court may take jurisdiction, even if the parents do not meet the residency requirements.

If a court declines jurisdiction or no home state exists, the courts may consider states where the child has significant connections. The UCCJEA framework prevents conflicting custody orders and discourages parents from relocating to obtain favorable custody rulings.

Establishing and Proving Residency

Most states require that you establish residency to file for divorce. Courts generally require a sworn statement plus supporting documentation. You must supply documentation to prove to the court that you meet the state's residency requirements. Commonly accepted forms of proof include:

- Driver's license or state-issued identification card
- Voter registration card
- Lease or rental agreements
- Utility bills for the past several months
- Military orders
- Vehicle registration
- Tax returns
- Employment records
- Bank statements
- Affidavits from third parties

Not all courts accept all types of documentation. Your attorney will let you know what is acceptable if you haven't changed your driver's license.

If you file an uncontested divorce, you will need these documents at the uncontested hearing to "prove up" the divorce.

Challenging Residency

Your spouse can challenge your residency. If he or she files a motion to that effect, and you cannot prove you have met the state's requirements, the court will most likely dismiss your case and require you to file in the appropriate jurisdiction.

Jurisdiction Issues

When both parties live in different states or counties, several jurisdictional issues could arise. If each party meets the residency requirements in other counties or states, either place may have jurisdiction. The location where the party first files for divorce will usually proceed with the case. However, some states may require that the petitioner file in the county or state where the defendant lives.

During an initial consultation, be sure to ask the attorney about jurisdiction. If the other party lives in a different county, the issue is not as complicated, since attorneys can usually practice in any state court, regardless of county, though it may cost you more because of travel time for the attorney.

However, living in a different state can pose a problem. The attorney must have a license to practice in the other state. If not, the attorney must file a *pro hac vice*[ii] motion and, in most cases, must work with a local attorney as "local counsel."

If you file in the incorrect jurisdiction, the court generally does not "transfer" cases. It will dismiss your case, and you will need to refile in the correct jurisdiction and pay the filing fees for that court. The court in the incorrect jurisdiction does not return your filing fee.

Uniform Child Custody Jurisdiction and Enforcement Act (UCCJEA) and a Child's "Home State"

The UCCJEA governs jurisdiction over child custody matters when parents live in different states or countries. The primary factor is the child's "home state." The UCCJEA defines this as the state where the child lived with the parent for at least six consecutive months immediately prior to the proceeding. If a child is under six months of age, the home state is where the child has lived since birth[iii].

If no state qualifies as the child's home state, courts may base jurisdiction on "significant connections," where the child has at least one parent who has strong ties to the state and substantial evidence regarding the child's care. In an emergency, if the child does not have a home state or a significant connection, a court can exercise temporary emergency jurisdiction to protect the child.

Once a court makes a valid custody determination under the UCCJEA, it retains exclusive, continuing jurisdiction until the child and both parents no longer have a significant connection to the state. Failing to meet the residency requirements of each state for divorce and the residency requirements for the child under the UCCJEA almost always results in a dismissal of the case, and the petitioner must refile in the appropriate jurisdiction.

CHAPTER 4: WAITING PERIODS

State laws often change. If you are filing *pro se*, be sure to conduct thorough research before filing. If you are working with an attorney, check with him or her for updated waiting periods for your state. Appendix II contains waiting periods as of June 2025.

Most states have a waiting period for obtaining a Final Judgment of Dissolution of Marriage (Divorce Decree, Final Judgment of Divorce) as created by state statute. A court will not finalize the divorce prior to the expiration of the waiting period.

In most cases, the waiting period starts on the date you file divorce papers, though some states may start the waiting period after the respondent receives the divorce papers. Some states require a longer waiting period if the parties have children.

The waiting period serves several purposes, including:

- **Cooling-Off Period**: A period of time for the parties to consider their decision, which reduces the likelihood of impulsive or emotionally driven divorce filings. It encourages the parties to think their actions through so they are fully aware of the consequences of filing for divorce.
- **Opportunity for Reconciliation**: The parties can use this time to attempt reconciliation, attend counseling or reconsider the consequences of ending the marriage.
- **Facilitates Negotiation and Settlement**: If the parties cannot or do not want to reconcile, the waiting period also allows them to negotiate and enter settlement

discussions, which significantly reduces the need for contentious litigation, which is time-consuming and costly.

- **Careful Consideration**: Finally, the waiting period ensures both parties have enough time to consider the legal, financial and emotional implications of divorce before the court finalizes it.

The waiting period also gives the parties and courts time to prepare for hearings and to address complex issues, including child custody and property division, in the hopes that they can reach a fair and thorough outcome.

Types of Waiting Periods

States generally follow one of two types of waiting periods: Post-filing and pre-filing. If your state has a post-filing waiting period, the time starts at the time you file the petition or on the date the process server serves your spouse. The post-filing period at the time you file the petition is the most common waiting period.

Some states use a pre-filing waiting period, which requires the spouses to live separately for a certain period of time prior to filing the petition. It is imperative that you document the separation date, especially if you do not ask the courts for a legal separation.

You can document a separation with proof of a notice of change of address, mail delivered to your new address—it will need the postmark for evidence, a signed lease agreement or documentation of putting utilities in your name at your new address.

You may also run into other procedural delays for specific issues, such as waiting for child custody evaluations, home studies, psychological evaluations or mandatory mediation. If the court requires any of the above, you may be able to complete them in a post-filing waiting period.

Exceptions and Modifications to the Waiting Period

Although waiting periods are a standard part of the divorce process, some cases may require an exception to or modification of the waiting period, which can significantly impact the divorce timeline and process, especially when the case involves custody issues. Understanding the exceptions and modifications can help the parties navigate the divorce process more effectively and ensure that they appropriately address urgent or unique circumstances.

Family Violence or Protective Orders

In cases that involve domestic violence, many states allow the courts to waive the mandatory waiting period to protect victims and their children from prolonged exposure to potentially dangerous situations.

If one party obtains an emergency protective order, whether a restraining order or an order of protection, it can be enough for the state to waive the mandatory waiting period without providing testimony and proof of domestic violence.

Obtaining a Waiting Period Waiver Without an Order of Protection

If a party needs a waiver of the waiting period due to domestic violence, but he or she does **_not_** have a restraining order or order of protection, the courts almost always require substantial evidence of abuse. The type and amount of proof vary from state to state. Typical forms of proof include:

- **Testimony**: The court often considers the victim's sworn testimony as evidence, especially if the testimony is specific and detailed.
- **Witness Statements**: Victims can also back up their testimony with testimony from friends, neighbors, family members and others who witnessed the abuse.
- **Medical Records**: Medical professionals must document evidence of domestic violence, including treatment.
- **Police Reports**: If the victim called the police during a domestic violence incident, law enforcement will have a report that you may be able to use as potential evidence. Some courts may require the responding officer to testify.
- **Photos or Videos**: Photos or videos, taken by you or others, including medical professionals and law enforcement, can often serve as evidence in some courts.
- **Communication**: Letters, voicemails, text messages, private messages on social media and emails can all serve as evidence in most cases. In most states, you cannot legally record a phone call without notifying the other party. If you need to record a phone conversation, speak with an attorney regarding your state's statutes regarding recording phone conversations.

Unlike criminal court, the accuser does not have to prove "beyond a reasonable doubt." Civil courts use "preponderance of the evidence," which means that the accuser must show that his or her claim is "more likely than not." This standard of proof is not as strict as the criminal court's beyond a reasonable doubt, where the accuser must prove the defendant's guilt to a degree that "no reasonable person would have a reasonable doubt" that the defendant committed the crime.

The Implications of Waiving or Modifying the Waiting Period in Custody Actions

In many cases involving domestic violence and/or protection orders, the courts issue temporary custody orders for the safety of the children. Depending on the situation, the orders may award

- Temporary sole custody to the alleged non-abusive parent
- Restrict or supervise the alleged abusive parent's visitation rights
- Prioritize the child's safety over standard procedural timelines, which can sometimes modify existing custody or visitation arrangements on an emergency basis.

Covenant Marriages

States that offer covenant marriages, including Arizona, Arkansas and Louisiana, often have longer waiting periods than standard marriages. In many cases, couples who enter into a covenant marriage agree to stricter requirements for entering and dissolving the marriage.

The laws may require the couple to attend counseling, demonstrate that they attempted to reconcile or provide specific grounds for divorce to reinforce the seriousness of the marital commitment.

This could affect custody arrangements, as the court may require additional mediation or counseling focused on the best interests of the children before it makes a final determination.

Modifications Related to Judicial Discretion

Most states have laws that give judges judicial discretion in modifying the waiting period in certain circumstances. The judge must have "good cause," which can include completed counseling, urgent needs, mediation or unique family situations.

The court may shorten the waiting period if both parties have resolved all issues and completed all required processes, or if they have compelling reasons, such as the health or safety of one of the parties or the child.

It can also extend the waiting period if the court determines the parties need more time for counseling, mediation or resolving complex custody or property issues.

The best interests of the child are the most common factor that guides judicial discretion. While family courts can be flexible, they rarely exhibit judicial discretion in circumstances that do not involve some form of domestic violence.

CHAPTER 5: LEGAL SEPARATION

Depending on your state's laws, you may informally separate or obtain a legal separation.

An **informal separation** is when both parties separate without a court order. Many states require a period of separation prior to entering a final judgment (divorce decree). Thus, when separating, remember the date that one of you moved out of the marital home.

Some states allow you to live in the same house as roommates, counting those days toward the period of informal or legal separation. However, you must live separate lives, and in most cases, you must be able to prove you lived separate lives.

A **legal separation** is one that the court orders. It often includes each party's rights and may encompass temporary child support, custody and time-sharing arrangements, spousal support, and property distribution.

Depending on your state, the rights of the parties may differ.

The Difference Between Legal Separation and Divorce

If the court orders a legal separation, you are still considered legally married, but you and your spouse live separately. You still have the same rights as you did while married. For example, you can still file joint taxes. Often, people who do not want to divorce for religious or insurance benefit reasons obtain a legal separation.

Reasons for Choosing Legal Separation

People may choose legal separation for a variety of reasons. First and foremost, deciding to divorce can be a difficult situation, even if both parties feel they can no longer live together. They may dread not only the divorce process but also the loss of potential stability that comes with the divorce becoming final.

Many people assume that divorce is the only way out of a marriage, and while that is true, you can sometimes have your cake and eat it, too. While you remain married while legally separated, you can also ask the court to create a parenting plan, divide assets, determine child support and divide property.

In some cases, it may be more advantageous for individuals to separate rather than obtain a divorce. In other cases, legal separation may cause nothing but trouble. If you are unsure which option is best for you, we recommend consulting with an attorney to review your options and rights in accordance with your state's laws.

Reasons people may prefer legal separation over divorce include:

Keeping Shared Benefits

When you choose to divorce, you will most likely lose access to certain financial benefits you enjoyed during the marriage, such as filing joint taxes, certain Social Security benefits, or employer-sponsored health insurance coverage.

Should you choose to ask for a legal separation, both parties can continue receiving these benefits while living apart.

- **Health Insurance**: In almost all cases, if you are on your spouse's health insurance, you will lose that benefit. While you can opt for COBRA, it is an expensive option that many cannot afford. Divorce *is* a qualifying life event, which means that you can obtain health insurance outside of the open enrollment period.

- **Social Security Benefits**: If you are age 62 and have been married for at least 10 years, you may be able to collect a portion of your ex-spouse's Social Security benefits.[iv] Your portion does not affect your ex-spouse's benefits, nor does it affect his or her current spouse's ability to claim your ex-spouse's benefits.
- **Military Benefits**: See Chapter 6 for military benefits.
- **Tax Advantages**: Once divorced, you can no longer file jointly. However, during a legal separation, because you are still legally married, you can file "Married, filing jointly."

Personal or Religious Beliefs

You may have personal or religious beliefs that view divorce as immoral. Obtaining a legal separation allows individuals with strict religious beliefs or personal values to remain married while living apart without potentially violating the code of conduct they follow.

Couples with young children may also wish to remain married to keep the family unit intact in the best interests of the children. However, if you do not get along with your spouse and argue over co-parenting, legal separation for the sake of the children could backfire on you.

Finally, in some cases, individuals may see divorce as a social stigma—something you can possibly avoid by opting for legal separation instead of divorce.

Financial Considerations / Government Benefit Programs

If you are close to meeting the 10-year requirement for Social Security benefits, **_and_** you will receive a higher benefit if you take part of your spouse's benefit, you may choose legal separation. You will need to review your spouse's Social Security benefit statement along with yours to determine which benefit is more beneficial.

Legal separation can also help you establish financial responsibilities and boundaries, such as determining how you will handle debts and whether you decide to maintain shared financial accounts.

We do recommend having your own bank accounts. If you are sharing debts, you can create a new shared account, and both spouses can deposit the amount required for his or her share of the debt. Both spouses have access to the account to ensure bills are paid on time, or that one spouse does not pay when the other has already paid.

Estate planning is another reason couples may opt for a legal separation rather than divorce. You can create separate wills and trusts while maintaining your inheritance rights. If you do not have a will, your estate will follow your state's succession laws. Generally, if you die intestate— without a will—your spouse receives your estate. Because you are still legally married, if you separate, your spouse will receive your entire estate unless the state you live in divides your estate between your spouse and children.

If you divorce, your next of kin is usually your living children, not your spouse.

Time to Reassess the Marriage

Divorce is usually an emotional time for couples, even if they agree they should divorce. However, the emotional situation also makes it harder to make the correct decisions. You may think you are ready to divorce in the heat of the moment, and may regret it later.

Legal separation allows you to live apart while remaining married, giving you time to reassess your choices and decisions. After a cooling-off period, many couples can repair their marriage. In some cases, being separated can make couples realize they still love each other and want to try again.

You can also take the time to prepare for the divorce by resolving financial and custodial disputes with less pressure before you decide that divorce is inevitable. During this time, you may choose to reconcile, remain legally separated or file for divorce.

Ultimately, a legal separation can be less stressful for children, as it allows for a gradual transition. Depending on their ages, a legal separation could reduce emotional stress for children. It gives children time to adjust to new living arrangements that may not be permanent and can help them transition to new parental roles.

Legal Effects of Separation on Divorce Issues

As with divorce, legal separation can have significant legal consequences. The terms of separation, whether informal or legal, often determine how courts address issues such as property division, spousal support and child custody.

The date of separation often determines which assets and debts are marital property or separate property and can influence the calculation of spousal and child support obligations.

Some jurisdictions require a mandatory separation period prior to granting a divorce. Understanding the effects of separation is essential, as these early decisions can have a lasting impact on the outcome of a divorce and your future financial and parental rights.

Property Distribution

Most states consider property purchased and debts incurred after the separation date as separate property; thus, the role of separation plays a critical role in classifying property during a divorce.

This distinction can significantly affect the division of real estate, retirement benefits, bank accounts and other assets. It can also affect who pays marital debts, including joint credit cards, loans and mortgages.

Child Custody and Support

Arrangements made during separation often become the starting point for custody and support decisions. Courts may consider the stability and suitability of custody and time-sharing schedules that you establish during the separation period when determining final orders. However, the court will always consider the best interests of the children before making new orders or agreeing to current schedules.

Additionally, the separation date can affect future child support orders. Typically, the non-custodial parent pays child support as soon as the parties separate. However, if the parties do not have a child support order in place or cannot prove voluntary child support payments, the court will order retroactive child support, which can be a significant amount, depending on the length of the separation.

When making voluntary child support payments, *always* write "Child support for [month, year] in the memo line.

Spousal Support

Separation can directly impact spousal support calculations. The duration of the separation may influence whether the court awards spousal support, as well as the amount and length of payments.

In some cases, spousal support arrangements you make during a separation, such as temporary spousal support, could set a precedent for support in the final divorce order.

States That Do Not Allow Legal Separation

Six states do not allow legal separation, though the parties may separate on their own:

- Delaware
- Florida
- Georgia
- Mississippi
- Pennsylvania
- Texas

The rest of the states may allow legal or informal separation or may require legal separation in order to obtain a divorce.

CHAPTER 6: MILITARY DIVORCE

Federal and state laws govern military divorce. Servicemembers and their spouses use civilian courts to get a divorce, just as civilians. However, servicemembers must have a clear understanding of federal and state laws.

Core issues, such as property division, child custody and support, and spousal support, remain central to the proceedings. Servicemembers must navigate additional complexities related to jurisdiction, residency and the division of military benefits.

Relocations, deployments and the mobile nature of military life often complicate decisions about where you need to file for divorce and how state laws apply to you.

Federal Laws Affecting Military Divorce

Two main laws apply to servicemembers filing for divorce: the Servicemembers Civil Relief Act (SCRA)[v] and the Uniformed Services Former Spouses' Protection Act (USFSPA)[vi]. These federal laws play a pivotal role in shaping the divorce process for servicemembers and their families. They provide protections and guidelines that exceed state statutes and directly impact how divorce proceedings unfold.

The SCRA shields active-duty servicemembers from legal disadvantages caused by military obligations, allows for delays in court proceedings and protects against default judgments if military duties prevent timely participation.

The USFSPA governs the division of military retirement benefits during divorce and permits civilian courts to award former spouses a fair share of these benefits, which are at least partially considered marital assets.

Servicemembers Civil Relief Act (SCRA)

Enacted in 2003, the Servicemembers Civil Relief Act protects the legal rights and financial interests of active-duty servicemembers. The Act is part of the Soldiers' and Sailors' Civil Relief Act of 1940. It covers all branches of the armed forces, certain commissioned corps and National Guard members called to active service for more than 30 consecutive days.

The Act does not eliminate debts or legal responsibilities; instead, it provides temporary relief and protections to ensure that servicemembers are not disadvantaged in civil matters due to their service.

Key Protections of the SCRA

Some of the most significant protections afforded to servicemembers[vii] under the SCRA include:

- **Stay of Proceedings**: Courts must postpone or suspend civil court or administrative proceedings if a servicemember's duties materially affect his or her ability to participate.
- **Protection Against Default Judgments**: A court cannot enter a default judgment against a servicemember without appointing an attorney to represent his or her interests and verifying the servicemember's military status.
- **Interest Rate Cap**: The SCRA limits interest rates on debts incurred prior to military service to 6 percent per year during active duty.
- **Eviction and Foreclosure Protections**: The Act prohibits foreclosures on mortgages and restricts evictions without a court order during the servicemember's active service.

- **Termination of Leases**: Allows servicemembers to terminate residential, automobile or business leases without incurring a penalty should the servicemember receive orders for a permanent change of station or deployment.
- **Stay of Execution on Judgments**: The Act allows the postponement of enforcement of judgments, attachments and garnishments against servicemembers.

Applicability and Duration

The SCRA protects the servicemember from the date he or she enters active duty and ends, in most cases, 90 days after discharge. It also extends some protection to dependents.

This federal law is an integral part of protecting a servicemember's legal and financial rights. Each servicemember contemplating divorce or who has been served with divorce should read the law to become familiar with his or her rights.

Uniformed Services Former Spouses' Protection Act (USFSPA)

In a nutshell, the USFSPA allows state courts to divide certain military benefits[viii] as marital property. It also governs the division of those assets. This federal law was enacted in 1982 to address the division of military pay and benefits during a divorce. Servicemembers should understand how the USFSPA affects them during divorce proceedings.

Legal Framework of the USFSPA

The Act authorizes state courts to treat disposable military retired pay as marital property, which means that courts can divide it in the event of a divorce, dissolution, annulment, or legal separation. Disposable retired pay includes the servicemember's monthly retired pay minus certain deductions, including disability pay.

The USFSPA does not guarantee that a former spouse shall receive any portion of the retired pay—it gives the courts discretion to award him or her a share based on the state's property division laws. It also allows state courts to enforce court-ordered child and spousal support through direct payments from the Defense Finance and Accounting Service (DFAS).

Procedural Requirements

- **Court Orders**: A former spouse must obtain a court order that specifically awards a portion of the pay as property. See 10/10 Rule.

- **Jurisdiction**: The state court must have jurisdiction over the servicemember by reason of residence other than because of military assignment, domicile or consent.

- **Enforcement**: DFAS can enforce court orders for the division of retired military pay and spousal and child support as long as the order meets the requirements of the USFSPA. The order must be final and must specify the amount or formula for division.

- **10/10 Rule[ix]**: The 10/10 requirement is often referred to as the "killer" requirement, as it bars spouses who do not meet the conditions of the rule from enforcing the award through direct payments from DFAS. In order to qualify, a spouse must have been married to the servicemember for at least 10 years, *and* the servicemember must have served for at least 10 years during that time.

- **20/20/20 Rule[x]**: If a servicemember served for at least 20 creditable years *and* the couple was married for at least 20 years, *and* the marriage overlapped the period of service by at least 20 years, the former spouse may continue receiving and using full commissary and exchange privileges and healthcare, as long as he or she does not remarry or have an employer-sponsored health plan.

- **20/20/15 Rule**: The former spouse may continue using health benefits for one year if the marriage lasted 20 years, the servicemember served 20 creditable years, *and* at least 15 of those years overlapped. After the first year, the spouse may purchase health insurance through DFAS. The 20/20/15 Rule also allows an ex-spouse to enjoy commissary access for one year after a divorce.

Practical Considerations

- **Retired Pay**: State courts determine the amount awarded to the former spouse, which can be up to 50 percent of the servicemember's disposable retired pay. If the order includes child and/or spousal support, the award can be up to 65 percent of the servicemember's disposable retired pay.

- **Medical, Commissary and Exchange Benefits**: Former spouses may qualify for continued benefits if the marriage and service overlap for at least 20 years (see 20/20/20 Rule). The former spouse may receive transitional benefits if he or she meets the 20/20/15 Rule.

- **Survivor Benefit Plan (SBP)**: A former spouse may be eligible for coverage under the SBP, which provides ongoing income after the servicemember's death.

Limitations and Special Cases

If the former spouse remarries, the marriage can affect certain benefits, including medical coverage and the Survivor Benefit Plan (SBP).

Navigating the Process

Because of the complexity of military divorce and the significant financial consequences, you should always consult with an experienced military family law attorney if you are ready to file for divorce or separate or if your spouse served you with divorce papers.

Your attorney should give you a chance to review any settlement agreement prior to submitting it to your spouse's attorney and should allow you to review the proposed final judgment prior to giving the court permission to execute it. Always read through those documents carefully, and be sure to ask questions if you do not understand something.

Why Some Say the USFSPA is Unfair to Servicemembers

Throughout your career, you may have heard that the USFSPA is unfair to servicemembers. Some issues may include:

Loss of Control Over Retirement Benefits

Because the USFSPA allows state courts to treat military retirement pay as marital property, some servicemembers view this as a loss of control over their own retirement savings. It can also be a detriment to the servicemember's financial security.

Potential for Unfairly High Award to Former Spouses

Critics argue that the USFSPA can often result in former spouses receiving a disproportionately large share of the servicemember's retirement pay (up to 65 percent), especially if the marriage was long-term or if the servicemember had a substantial military career.

Unforeseen Consequences

Some critics of the USFSPA argue that the Act may create financial difficulties for servicemembers attempting to transition to civilian life, as the division of retirement pay can affect the servicemember's ability to save and invest for the future.

CHAPTER 7: PROPERTY DIVISION

Most states adhere to the legal theory of equitable distribution for property division, whether for divorce proceedings or legal separation. The nine states that adhere to community property laws include Arizona, California, Idaho, Louisiana, Nevada, New Mexico, Texas, Washington and Wisconsin.

Whether your state uses equitable distribution or community property laws, they significantly affect how you divide marital property during a divorce.

Regardless of whether your state is an equitable distribution or community property state, it considers certain property as separate property, which the courts do not divide in a divorce.

Separate Property vs. Marital Property

Determining what is separate and what is marital property can often be straightforward, or it can be very complex. What you think might be yours alone may be marital property if you commingled (mixed) the property by using marital funds for maintenance or upkeep, or by depositing the separate property into a marital account.

The basic rules are:

- If you owned it prior to the marriage, it may be separate property if you did not put your spouse's name on the deed, title or account, deposit it into a joint account, or use joint funds to maintain it.
- If you purchased it after you separated, it may be separate property unless you used marital funds for the purchase.

However, if you use marital funds—money earned or received during the marriage—to make payments or maintain the property, whether it is real estate or personal property, the courts may consider it marital property regardless of whose name is on the deed, title or account.

Most states count inheritances and gifts received during the marriage as separate property. However, if you commingled assets, including cash, from the inherited property or gift, it may become marital property.

Finally, any property included in a prenuptial or postnuptial agreement usually remains separate property. However, you must be able to show that neither party was under duress at the time of signing it and that it meets state law requirements, including whether you executed the document correctly.

Equitable Distribution of Property

If your state's laws use equitable distribution, your spouse does not automatically receive half of the marital property during the divorce. Instead, the division is equitable based on several factors. You might receive 60 or 70 percent of the marital property, or you might receive 30 or 40 percent, depending on your spouse's financial position; thus, the term "equitable." It is not necessarily equal, although the court could order a 50-50 split if both of your financial positions are relatively equal.

Factors Determining Equitable Distribution of Property

While each state's laws are different, the most common factors that courts review when determining equitable distribution include:

- The duration of the marriage
- Each spouse's current and future financial circumstances and needs
- Income disparity

- The earning potential of each spouse after the divorce

- The standard of living established during the marriage

- Contributions of each spouse to the marriage, including homemaking, childcare and financial contributions

- Contributions to the other spouse's career advancement

- Contributions to the other spouse's education

- The interruption of one spouse's career for the benefit of the marriage or family

- The value of each spouse's separate (nonmarital) property

- The economic circumstances of each party at the time of division

- The desirability of awarding the marital home or the right to live there to the spouse who receives custody of the children

- Wasting or hiding of assets by one or the other spouse

- The debts and liabilities of each spouse

- Tax consequences of the property distribution

- Any written agreements between the parties, including prenuptial or postnuptial agreements

Process for Identifying, Valuing and Dividing Assets and Debts

Equitable distribution of assets and liabilities during a divorce involves several steps:

Identifying the Assets and Liabilities

During the discovery process, you will need to compile a comprehensive inventory of assets and liabilities owned by both parties, whether jointly or in one or the other's name. This includes bank accounts, real estate, retirement funds, vehicles, personal property, business interests and outstanding debt. **All states require both parties to disclose all assets and liabilities.**

Classifying Property

Once you complete the inventory, your attorney will assist you in classifying the property and debts as either marital or separate.

Valuing Assets and Debts

Once you classify assets and liabilities as marital or separate, you must assign each a fair market value. You may need to retain professional appraisers for certain items, such as the marital home, antiques, jewelry, or businesses, to obtain a true and fair valuation.

Negotiating a Settlement or Court Intervention

You can attempt to settle property division through mutual agreement, negotiation or mediation. If you and your spouse can come to an agreement, your attorney will draft a settlement agreement, even if you have other outstanding issues.

If you cannot reach an agreement, the court will intervene and make a final decision based on your state's laws and the previously listed factors.

Dividing Assets and Liabilities

The final step is the actual division of assets as dictated in your marital settlement agreement or court order. In many cases, the parties have already divided their personal property if they are separated.

If you do not feel safe retrieving your property from the marital home or allowing your spouse into the marital home to pick up his or her property, you can ask a police officer or a friend to accompany you. This is common in cases of domestic violence.

If you have an active protective order against you (or you have one against your spouse), you should bring a police officer with you; otherwise, the court could see it as a violation of the protective order.

In some cases, you may not need another person or police officer with you as long as the court has ordered a specific date and time to pick up your belongings or exchange other property; however, we recommend that you do have someone with you due to the protective order.

Community Property Division

In community property states—Arizona, California, Idaho, Louisiana, Nevada, New Mexico, Texas, Washington, and Wisconsin—state laws consider all assets and liabilities acquired by either spouse during the marriage to be jointly owned and subject to equal distribution during divorce.

As with equitable distribution states, assets in community property states include income earned during the marriage, real and personal property, retirement accounts, and debts incurred during the marriage, including those in the name of either spouse.

Separate property includes assets and liabilities owned by one spouse prior to the marriage. It also includes gifts and inheritances. If the property or liability has been commingled in such a way that makes it indistinguishable, it becomes marital property.

Dividing Marital Property in Community Property States

In a community property state, the law typically requires the parties to divide all community assets and debts equally rather than equitably. Some states, such as California, enforce a strict equal division, while others, like Texas, allow courts to make "just and right" adjustments, although the presumption remains equal division unless there are compelling reasons to deviate.

Community property laws also treat debts incurred during the marriage as community obligations and split them equally, regardless of which spouse incurred the debt.

Treatment of Commingled and Complex Assets

Commingled property arises when couples mix separate assets with community assets, such as depositing an inheritance, which is separate property, into a joint account or using marital funds to pay down a mortgage on a home one of the parties owns separately.

When parties commingle assets, the original separate property may become community property unless the owner can trace and prove the source of the funds or assets used to maintain the separate property.

Complex assets, such as retirement accounts, are also subject to community property rules. For example, the portion of a retirement account accrued during the marriage is community property and subject to equal division. When this happens, you often need a Qualified Domestic Relations Order (QDRO)[xi] to split the account without tax penalties.

If an account contains separate and community contributions, you may have to retain a forensic accountant to determine how much of the account is separate property and how much is community property. In some cases, courts may consider everything from the date of marriage to the date of separation or divorce as community property and everything outside of those dates as separate property. However, you would need to know the exact date of your marriage, separation, or entry of the divorce decree.

CHAPTER 8: BUSINESS AND DIVORCE

Business interests play a pivotal role in divorce proceedings and can significantly complicate the process, especially when both parties have a stake in the business. These assets often represent a significant portion of the marital estate and are usually difficult to value and divide, as companies are dynamic, and their value can fluctuate. They also often involve tangible and intangible elements, such as reputation and goodwill.

The valuation and division of business assets require specialized knowledge and careful consideration of business and personal finances to ensure a fair outcome for both spouses.

All businesses, especially family-owned or closely held companies, pose unique challenges because of the incorporation documents, state laws, tax laws and more. The divorce process that includes a business often takes much longer than a divorce process for a couple who does not own or hold an interest in a business.

Valuing a Business Interest in Divorce

The first step in property division for a business is valuing the real estate and holdings. An accurate valuation is critical for equitable asset division. It is not a simple appraisal, such as you would see for personal real estate. The process includes:

- Reviewing financial statements, tax returns and other relevant documents for three to five years
- Retaining a business valuation specialist, whether appointed by the parties or the court

A business specialist can create a valuation by using one of the following approaches:

- **Asset**: The specialist calculates a value based on the business's assets minus liabilities.
- **Income**: The specialist, often a forensic accountant, focuses on the earning potential of the business using projected future income to estimate its present value.
- **Market**: A specialist can also use the market approach, which compares the business to similar businesses that have recently sold.
- **Discounted Cash Flow**: This method estimates the present value of expected future cash flows and discounts it to reflect risk and the time value of money.

A valuator also considers certain intangible factors, such as reputation, customer loyalty and goodwill. The choice of method depends on several factors, including the nature of the business, specific divorce circumstances, and the business's financial structure.

Because neutrality and transparency are crucial to a fair division, a neutral third-party valuation is preferred to ensure fairness and minimize disputes.

The Role of Business Valuation Specialists

Courts may require the parties to retain impartial, qualified business valuation experts to ensure fairness and accuracy in the valuation process. In many cases, the parties will seek out these specialists on their own to ensure a fair division of assets and liabilities.

If the parties cannot agree on a neutral third-party appraiser, the court may appoint its own experts.

Key Factors Affecting Business Valuation

Many factors can affect business valuation, including:

- The historical and projected financial performance
- Prevailing market conditions
- Company-specific risks
- Discretionary expenses
- Normalization adjustments
- Officer compensation
- Intangible assets, such as your customer base, reputation and goodwill
- Transparency and accuracy of financial records, imperative for a defensible valuation
- Timing of valuation due to business fluctuations

Options to Consider for Dividing Business Assets

Once the valuation expert values the business, you must decide how to divide the assets. The most common options include:

- **Buyout**: One spouse retains the business and compensates the other for his or her share, either through a lump-sum payment or structured payments over time.
- **Co-Ownership**: Both spouses continue to own and operate the business together after the divorce. This option is rare and typically only pursued when both parties have a strong working relationship and mutual trust. Even so, issues can arise later.
- **Selling the Business**: Sell the business to a third party and divide the proceeds according to the court's order or your settlement agreement.
- **Offsetting Assets**: You can "trade" assets, such as real estate or investment accounts of an equivalent value, to achieve equitable distribution.

The method you choose depends on the business's liquidity, the preference of both parties and the practicality of ongoing joint ownership. Each option has unique tax implications and liquidity challenges that the parties must carefully evaluate during settlement negotiations.

Special Considerations for Family-Owned or Closely Held Businesses

Closely held and family-owned businesses present unique challenges during the divorce process. These businesses often lack a market for shares, which makes valuation more complex and sometimes contentious.

Special considerations include:

- **Control and Management**: Determine which spouse will continue to manage the business once the divorce is finalized, especially if both spouses are actively involved in the business.
- **Minority Discounts**: If one spouse receives a minority interest, lack of control or marketability may become discounted.
- **Impact on Family and Employees**: The division of the business will most likely affect other family members and employees who depend on the business for their livelihood.
- **Succession Planning**: The divorce will most likely necessitate changes in succession plans or the business structure, especially if children or extended family members are involved in the business.

Depending on the divorce circumstances and other factors, you may be able to work out a creative solution with careful planning that addresses these challenges while preserving the business's viability and ensuring both parties receive their fair share.

Legal and Strategic Issues

Your decisions—or the court's decision—have several legal and strategic issues. Because of the complexity of dividing a business and how it can impact your future financial security, consider retaining a business attorney to collaborate with your family law attorney (unless your family law attorney also has extensive business law experience) to lead negotiations.

Some legal and strategic issues you should consider when determining the best course of action for business valuation and division include:

- **Disclosure Requirements and Risks of Misrepresentation**: You must provide full disclosure of the business finances, as failing to do so can result in legal penalties and an unfair settlement, which may lead the court to believe you are hiding assets. This, in turn, could affect spousal support awards and the division of personal property percentages.
- **Handling Valuation and Division Disputes**: Be ready for disagreements. You can potentially resolve these issues through mediation prior to court intervention.
- **The Role of Professional Advisors**: Business appraisers, forensic accountants and experienced legal counsel are essential for navigating complex business valuations and ensuring compliance with state laws.
- **State-Specific Legal Standards**: The laws governing business division in divorce vary from state to state, and that influences valuation standards and division methods.

Tips for a Smoother Business Valuation and Division Process

Proper business valuation is crucial for achieving a fair outcome in your divorce case. You can mitigate the risk of an unfair split by:

- Assembling and organizing all business financial records as soon as possible, even prior to filing for divorce.
- Selecting experienced valuation experts with the proper credentials to ensure the valuation is objective and defensible.
- Being flexible during settlement negotiations.
- Considering tax and liquidity impacts.
- Taking steps to protect business operations during and after the divorce, such as updating ownership agreements and clarifying roles.

CHAPTER 9: BANKRUPTCY AND DIVORCE

It is common for couples to file for bankruptcy at the same time or shortly after they file their divorce case. Financial hardship is one of the leading contributors to marital breakdown, and the divorce process can exacerbate or even trigger financial instability. In these cases, one or both spouses may seek bankruptcy protection.

When these legal processes overlap, they can create unique challenges, including determining how to divide marital assets and debts, handling child and spousal support obligations and navigating the impact of the bankruptcy's automatic stay on divorce proceedings.

Because different courts and sets of laws govern bankruptcy and family law, combining the two processes can often lead to confusion, delays and unintended financial consequences if you do not carefully manage them. We suggest that if you plan to file for bankruptcy while going through the divorce process, you retain a family law attorney with extensive experience in bankruptcy proceedings.

How Bankruptcy Affects Divorce Proceedings

Filing for bankruptcy during the divorce process can significantly affect the divorce, primarily due to the automatic stay that takes effect as soon as you file a Notice of Bankruptcy. The stay stops all court actions to obtain or control property of the bankruptcy estate, which includes most marital property.

Because of the stay, the family court usually cannot proceed with dividing assets until the bankruptcy court grants permission to continue or the bankruptcy is discharged. However, the automatic stay does not apply to child custody and child support proceedings[xii].

The Impact of Bankruptcy on Support Obligations and Property Settlements

Bankruptcy does not discharge domestic support obligations, such as spousal support and child support. Regardless of any bankruptcy proceeding, these obligations remain enforceable, which means that the automatic stay does not affect them.

However, bankruptcy can impact a spouse's ability to pay support, especially if it reduces their financial resources.

Additionally, depending on whether you file Chapter 7 (liquidation) or Chapter 13 (reorganization), property settlement obligations, such as payments required to equalize asset division, may be treated differently if they are part of the divorce decree.

If you file Chapter 7, you cannot discharge property settlement obligations in most circumstances. However, if you file Chapter 13, you may be able to discharge certain property settlement debts[xiii].

Bankruptcy and Divorce Are Separate Legal Processes

Bankruptcy is a federal legal process that helps people manage overwhelming debt. The two most common types of bankruptcy are Chapter 7 and Chapter 13.

Chapter 7 liquidates all of your assets and discharges most unsecured debts, such as medical bills and credit cards, usually within four to seven months. In exchange, the bankruptcy trustee sells nonexempt assets to pay creditors, though those who file may keep a lot of their property due to exemptions.

Chapter 13 reorganizes debt. Debtors keep their assets but must propose a repayment plan, which typically lasts three to five years. Depending on the debtor's disposable income, he or she (or a couple, in the case of spouses filing jointly) pays some or all of the debt back over time.

Filing Chapter 13 allows debtors to catch up on secured debts such as mortgages or car loans while discharging unsecured debts at the end of the plan.

Whereas bankruptcy is a federal court process, divorce is a state court process that ends a marriage and addresses key issues such as asset and debt division, child and spousal support, child custody and timesharing.

Although divorce and bankruptcy are separate legal actions, their outcomes can significantly impact each other, especially regarding the division of debts, the financial stability of both parties and support obligations after the divorce.

Timing: Which Comes First?

The timing of bankruptcy and divorce filings can significantly affect the outcome of both processes. Filing both requires you to carefully assess your financial situation, the nature of your debts and your relationship with your spouse. Then, you need to determine whether filing for bankruptcy before, during or after the divorce best fits your circumstances.

The Pros and Cons of Filing Bankruptcy Prior to, During or After Divorce

Filing for bankruptcy prior to filing for divorce can simplify the division of assets and liabilities since you may be able to discharge joint debts. Additionally, you can also share legal fees. Using this approach can often make the divorce process smoother because you reduce the number of financial issues that you need to resolve as part of the divorce.

However, it can delay the divorce because the bankruptcy's automatic stay could pause property division until the bankruptcy case concludes—and for Chapter 13 cases, this could be up to five years unless the bankruptcy court allows you to lift the stay pertaining to asset division.

Filing for bankruptcy during the divorce process can cause delays and complications with asset division, so many attorneys do not recommend it. However, in some cases, it is inevitable, as the parties may lose the marital home if they do not file.

Filing for bankruptcy after divorce allows each party to address their own financial situation, but it could result in higher legal costs and lower exemption limits. Additionally, the bankruptcy court will not discharge support obligations.

Filing Joint Bankruptcy vs. Filing Separate Bankruptcy

You can save on legal fees and maximize exemptions if you file a joint bankruptcy with your spouse. However, it requires cooperation, which may not be feasible if your relationship is contentious. Filing separately during or after divorce gives each spouse more control, but it could increase costs and limit the amount of property that the bankruptcy protects from creditors.

When it comes down to the wire, the best approach depends on the couple's financial circumstances, the types of debt they have, and their ability to work together. It is essential that you consult with a family law attorney and a bankruptcy attorney (or one who has extensive experience in both areas of law).

The Automatic Stay and Its Effects on Divorce Cases

The automatic stay is a fundamental bankruptcy protection law that takes effect as soon as you file a Notice of Bankruptcy or the bankruptcy petition. It is a legal injunction that stops most collection actions by your creditors.

Because a creditor must cease collection efforts, you have a little breathing room to make important financial decisions and organize your finances. If a creditor continues to pursue collections, refer it to your bankruptcy attorney. Creditors cannot continue efforts to file lawsuits, garnish wages, initiate or continue foreclosure proceedings, or harass you over the phone, via regular mail, or through digital contact means.

The "lifting of the stay" means the bankruptcy court gives permission for the creditor to resume collections, or in the case of a family law case, it could permit the parties to negotiate a settlement or litigate property division.

How the Stay Delays Divorce Proceedings

The automatic stay can significantly impact divorce proceedings, especially when it comes to dividing marital property. Once you file for bankruptcy, the stay generally prevents the continuation or initiation of legal actions to obtain or control property of the bankruptcy estate, which usually includes marital assets that are subject to division in a divorce.

Courts may be unable to proceed with property division until you resolve the bankruptcy case or the bankruptcy court grants relief from the stay, which would then allow the family court to move forward with these matters. If the bankruptcy court does not approve lifting the stay for the divorce case, it will delay the finalization of the divorce.

Exceptions for Domestic Support Obligations

The automatic stay does ***not*** apply to all aspects of divorce. Actions to establish or modify child or spousal support, as well as the collection of ongoing support obligations, are almost always exempt from the stay. A former spouse or a child support agency can pursue collections of these obligations without violating the stay, ensuring the bankruptcy process does not interrupt essential support for children and the former spouse.

Special Issues and Strategic Considerations

Some of the special issues and strategic considerations you should take into account and discuss with your attorney include:

- If one spouse files for bankruptcy and has a joint debt discharged, the creditor can still initiate collections against the other spouse.
- Include an indemnification clause in the divorce. It states that one spouse must hold the other harmless for joint debts assigned to one spouse.
- When dividing assets and debts, divide them in a way that ensures the spouse receiving the asset also receives the corresponding debt.
- When one spouse takes on a joint debt, that spouse should refinance the debt in their own name only. If that is not possible, you may want to reconsider the division of assets so that the spouse who *can* pay the debt receives the asset.

- If you have debts held in one spouse's name only, that spouse should take that debt.

CHAPTER 10: CHILD CUSTODY

Child custody is one of the most significant and emotionally charged issues in family law. When parents divorce or separate, custody often becomes a central issue in the legal process. Custody arrangements not only affect your rights as parents but can have lasting impacts on the well-being and stability of children.

In all states, the law recognizes that children's best interests guide custody decisions. Courts consider a wide range of factors to ensure custody arrangements support the child's physical, emotional and developmental needs. These decisions include legal custody, which is the right to make major decisions about education, religion and healthcare, and physical custody—the child's living arrangements and daily care.

Understanding the legal framework and principles behind custody is imperative, as it significantly impacts the parent-child relationship, family dynamics and the child's future.

Types of Custody

Courts order two main types of custody, further divided into subtypes. When you divorce or separate, determining custody involves several types of custody arrangements, including:

Legal Custody

The right and responsibility to make major decisions about the child's upbringing, including choices related to education, healthcare, religion and extracurricular activities, is legal custody. Parents can have sole or joint legal custody.

If the court orders sole legal custody, only one parent has decision-making authority and does not need consent from the other parent.

Joint legal custody allows both parents to share in decision-making responsibilities. They must communicate and cooperate on major issues affecting the child.

Because it is generally in the best interests of the child for both parents to remain involved, joint legal custody is more common than sole legal custody. The court will only order sole legal custody if it determines that one parent is unable to make reasonable decisions, a parent is incarcerated, or, in some extreme cases, the parents are unable to work together to co-parent.

Physical Custody

The other half of custody is physical custody—where the child lives and which parent provides daily care. Physical custody can also be sole or joint. If a parent has sole physical custody, the child lives primarily with one parent, who is responsible for day-to-day care. The other parent usually has visitation or parenting time rights, frequently referred to as "time sharing."

If the parties have joint physical custody, the child spends a significant amount of time living with both parents. However, this is not necessarily a 50/50 split. This arrangement requires coordination and cooperation between the parents to maintain stability for the child.

Split Custody

When each parent has custody of one or more children in families with multiple children, they have split custody. This arrangement is not as common because courts usually avoid separating siblings unless the parents agree or there are compelling reasons.

Split custody can also refer to arrangements where children alternate living with each parent on a rotating basis, such as "bird's nest[xiv]" custody, where the children remain in the family home and the parents take turns living there.

Exclusive Custody

When one parent has sole legal and physical custody, he or she has exclusive custody. The courts award exclusive custody if they find that the other parent is not fit or is unable to care for the child due to safety concerns or incapacity. This type of custody limits the other parent's involvement, sometimes restricting visitation or decision-making rights.

50/50 Co-Parenting and Equal Time Sharing

Equal shared parenting is an increasingly common custody arrangement in which both parents share nearly equal physical custody of their children, allowing them to spend substantial time living with each parent. Both parents participate in day-to-day parenting decisions (legal custody).

Equal shared parenting may not be suitable for every family. However, if the parents can make it work, it has significant benefits for the children.

Benefits of 50/50 Co-Parenting

If the parents can effectively co-parent despite their differences, equal shared parenting has many benefits for the children, including:

- **Strong Relationships with Both Parents**: Children benefit from meaningful, ongoing relationships with both parents, which can foster emotional security and stability.
- **Promotes Stability**: Equal time sharing can reduce the children's feelings of loss after divorce and help maintain continuity in their lives.
- **Encourages Cooperative Parenting**: Parents must communicate and collaborate regularly, which can improve co-parenting dynamics and shared responsibility.
- **Gender-Neutral Parenting**: This arrangement supports evolving family roles, allowing both parents to remain fully involved in the children's lives.
- **Potential Emotional and Psychological Benefits**: Children in joint custody arrangements often experience better emotional and psychological outcomes than those in sole custody situations.

Challenges and Considerations of Equal Shared Parenting

Despite the benefits of 50/50 custody, it does have challenges. Both parents must take several factors into consideration.

- **High Levels of Cooperation Required**: In order for equal shared parenting to be beneficial to the children, this custody arrangement necessitates effective communication and a willingness to cooperate. High-conflict relationships or poor communication can undermine the arrangement and negatively affect the children.

- **Logistical Complexities**: Frequent transitions between two homes can be challenging for children and parents, especially when parents live far apart or have differing schedules.

- **Consistency and Routine**: Maintaining consistent rules, routines and expectations across two households can be difficult, potentially causing confusion or stress for children.

- **Financial Implications**: Supporting two homes suitable for children may result in increased expenses. Equal shared parenting can impact child support calculations, typically resulting in lower payments, depending on each parent's income and the specifics of the arrangement.

- **Not Suitable for All Families**: Equal shared parenting may not work well in cases involving high conflict, domestic violence or when one parent is unable to provide a stable environment.

Court Considerations for Equal Shared Parenting

In order for a court to consider equal shared parenting, it must believe that the arrangement is in the best interests of the children. The court considers several factors in assessing the feasibility of 50/50 co-parenting, including:

Parents' Work Schedules

Both parents must have the ability to provide care during their parenting time. Those who work swing shifts or frequently travel for work may not benefit from equal shared parenting, as it may not be in the child's best interests.

Proximity of Residences

When both parents live near each other, 50/50 custody is much easier, as the child's school is closer to the parents. Otherwise, the parent who lives outside the school district would have to travel to bring the child to school and pick him or her up. This extra travel time could interfere with the parent's work schedule, and it decreases the amount of quality time the parent spends with the child.

Child's Needs and Preferences

The equal shared custody arrangement must suit the child's age, temperament and specific needs.

Parents' Ability to Communicate

Both parents must have excellent communication skills and must be able to cooperate and resolve conflicts in the child's best interests.

The Best Interests of the Child Standard

The "best interests of the child" standard is the guiding principle courts use when making custody decisions and divorce and separation cases. This standard ensures that all custody arrangements prioritize the child's welfare, safety and overall well-being rather than the preferences or convenience of the parents.

Whether the parents can agree on custody arrangements or the court decides, the child's best interests remain the central focus. When parents create a parenting plan for custody and visitation, the court will only approve it if it determines that the plan is in the child's best interests. Thus, parents creating their own parenting plan must always keep this standard at the forefront when agreeing on custody arrangements.

Common Factors Courts Consider When Determining the Child's Best Interests

The courts consider several factors when determining what is in the child's best interests. It does not make a decision based on a single factor but rather on the totality of the circumstances.

The goal is to foster a nurturing environment that allows the child to emotionally and physically thrive.

While specific factors may vary by state, courts generally evaluate a broad set of considerations to determine what arrangements will best serve the child's needs, including:

The Child's Relationship with Each Parent

The court considers several factors in the child's relationship with each parent, including the strength, nature, and stability of the child's bond. It also examines which parent has been more involved in the child's daily care and nurturing, including taking the child to doctor's appointments, attending school meetings and functions, and participating in extracurricular activities.

The Child's Wishes

Depending on the child's age and maturity, the court may ask the child about his or her preferences regarding living arrangements. However, this is only part of the consideration. The court may ask the child to appear *in camera,* a private meeting between the judge and the child, so that the child does not feel he or she must respond in one way or another to please one or the other parent.

The Parents' Mental and Physical Health

The physical and psychological well-being of each parent plays a vital role in determining custody. Each parent must be able to provide a safe, supportive environment for the child to thrive.

Stability and Continuity of the Home Environment

Courts will almost always favor arrangements that maintain consistency in the child's life, such as staying in the same home, school or community, to lessen the disruptive impact of divorce as much as possible.

Special Needs and How Each Parent Addresses Them During and After the Marriage

If a child has unique medical, educational, or emotional needs, the court examines each parent's ability and willingness to meet those needs. This may include spending extra one-on-one time with the child, taking the child to doctor's appointments, and attending necessary therapy sessions, including physical, psychological, cognitive, and occupational therapies.

History of Abuse, Substance Use or Domestic Violence

One of the most weighted considerations is whether there is any evidence of abuse, neglect, substance abuse or domestic violence by the parent, as the child's safety is paramount.

Adjustment to School or Community

The court will review adjustments and prospects for stability in the child's school and community when determining custody arrangements that are in the child's best interests.

Sibling and Extended Family Relationships

Courts recognize the value of maintaining strong sibling bonds and relationships with extended family, such as grandparents and step-siblings, and will weigh the benefits of moving out of the area or remaining in the same community when determining custody arrangements.

CHAPTER 11: VISITATION (TIME SHARING)

Visitation is a fundamental aspect of family law that ensures non-custodial parents maintain meaningful relationships with their children after a divorce or separation. It can also apply to others, although it is most common for grandparents to request visitation. Visitation focuses on the time and manner in which a non-custodial parent or other party spends time with the child.

Ongoing contact with both parents is, in most cases, beneficial to the children, except in cases where the safety of the child is at risk.

The Legal Basis of Visitation

The court typically grants visitation rights to the non-custodial parent. These rights stem from the parent-child relationship, and the court strongly presumes these rights unless it finds that visitation would be harmful to the child.

The court may impose restrictions, such as supervised visitation or may even deny visitation in cases with a history of abuse, neglect or severe mental illness. However, the court prefers that, as long as the child is safe, he or she has the ability to visit the non-custodial parent to foster a strong relationship.

Visitation is distinct from legal and physical custody, allowing the non-custodial parent to spend time with the child. The non-custodial parent may have joint legal and/or physical custody with the custodial parent, but if he or she does not have legal custody, that parent does not have the right to make decisions for the minor child.

Types of Visitation

The court generally orders four types of visitation, including no visitation at all. Non-custodial parents can request that the court modify the type of visitation originally ordered. If a court enters temporary orders for a specific kind of visitation, it often orders the same type of visitation in the final divorce decree.

Types of visitation include:

Standard Visitation

Most visitation arrangements follow a regular schedule. A common visitation schedule includes alternating weekends, holidays and birthdays. Structured schedules that include holidays, birthdays and other special days provide consistency and predictability for the child and the parents.

An example might include:

- Every other weekend, from Friday at 6:00 pm until Sunday at 6:00 pm.
- One weeknight every other week, from after school until it's time for the child to go to school in the morning.
- Thanksgiving on even years for one spouse and odd years for the other.
- Christmas falls on even years for the spouse who has Thanksgiving on odd years, and vice versa.
- Birthdays are split in half, i.e., one parent has the child on the child's birthday in the morning on odd years, and the other has the child in the morning on even years.
- Spring and winter breaks are split in half, or they may alternate in the same manner that Christmas and Thanksgiving rotate.
- Rotating major holidays other than Christmas and Thanksgiving.
- Father's Day spent with Dad, and Mother's Day is spent with Mom.

Some families include the parents' birthdays in the schedule.

Supervised Visitation

If the court believes that a child's safety is at risk while with a parent, it can order supervised visitations. If a parent has supervised visitation, he or she must exercise his or her visitation rights in the presence of a third party.

The third party may be a trusted friend or relative with whom both parents agree, or it may be someone appointed by the court, typically through a court program.

Some people consider arrangements to exchange the child in public as a form of supervised visitation, although technically, it is not. If you have a history of domestic violence or have a propensity to fly off the handle at your spouse but not your child, the court may order you to exchange the child at a police station or a very busy public area.

The court may order public exchanges even without a history of domestic violence if your spouse requests it because he or she no longer trusts being alone with you.

Virtual Visitation

Some courts may allow or encourage virtual visitation via phone calls, video chats or other electronic means, especially when parents live far apart.

No Visitation

In some cases, the court may deny visitation if it finds clear evidence that any contact with the non-custodial parent would put the child in danger or if the non-custodial parent is incarcerated.

Parenting Time Arrangements (Visitation Schedules)

Parenting time arrangements support the child's relationship with both parents after divorce or separation. You can follow any of the typical schedules or customize them to fit your situation as long as your schedule is in the best interests of the child.

Examples of Common Parenting Time Arrangements

Some people have different work hours. They may work nights or be in the military and have to schedule visitation around deployments. Do not feel that you have to choose a "typical" visitation schedule.

Week-On/Week-Off

This schedule is a typical schedule when the parties have equal time sharing. It works best when the parents live relatively close to each other. The child alternates between each parent's home on a weekly basis.

The parents also rotate holidays. One parent has the child for Christmas on even-numbered years and Thanksgiving on odd-numbered years, and the other parent has Christmas on odd-numbered years and Thanksgiving on even-numbered years. They also arrange other holidays in the same manner, e.g., Memorial Day and Independence Day (July 4th).

You can pair any two holidays or simply rotate the holidays yearly.

Alternating Weekends Plus Midweek Visits

This schedule is very common for "regular" visitation. The child lives primarily with one parent and visits the other every other weekend, usually from Friday after school until Sunday evening. The child also spends one midweek overnight or evening with the non-custodial parent.

2-2-3 and 3-4-4-3 Schedules

The child spends two days with one parent, two days with the other, and then three days with the first parent, repeating this rotation each week.

Week 1: Mom for two days, Dad for two days, Mom for three days

Week 2: Dad for two days, Mom for two days, Dad for three days

Repeat Week 1

Repeat Week 2

The 3-4-4-3 schedule is based on the same premise, but the schedule splits time over a two-week cycle, giving each parent nearly equal time.

First two weeks: Mom for three days, Dad for four days, Mom for four days, Dad for three days

Second two weeks: Repeat the first two weeks.

Holiday and Vacation Rotations

Regardless of the type of visitation schedule you create, there are special rules for holidays, school breaks, and summer vacations to ensure that both parents share important times with the child.

Most parents rotate holidays and split extended breaks evenly. Many also add special days to the list:

- **Child's Birthday**: Can rotate yearly or split the day in half.
- **Mother's Birthday**: Spent with the mother every year.
- **Father's Birthday**: Spent with the father every year.
- **Mother's Day**: Spent with the mother every year.
- **Father's Day**: Spent with the father every year.

Other Custom Arrangements

Some families use first, third and fifth weekend schedules, long weekends or daytime-only visitation, especially when overnight stays are not appropriate.

The Importance of Flexibility and Stability

Consistency is essential, but parents must also remain flexible. Changing needs, such as school events, parents' work schedules, and extracurricular activities, may require adjustments. Rigid schedules are not always in the child's best interests, so parents should communicate openly and adjust as necessary.

Being flexible also reduces conflict and allows families to adapt as their children grow and circumstances evolve. For example, if your child is in a school play or on the football team, and your work schedule does not allow you to get the child to the event, allowing the other parent to have a few hours of visitation during your time shows goodwill and flexibility.

Parenting Coordination or Mediation

Sometimes, parents disagree about visitation schedules, especially when the needs of the family change. Parenting coordinators and mediators are professionals who can help parents resolve disputes and develop workable solutions without returning to court.

These services can be invaluable for families experiencing high conflict or when communication breaks down, ensuring the child's needs remain the priority and that both parents' rights are respected and intact.

Restrictions and Enforcement

In certain circumstances, courts may restrict visitation or require supervised visitation if credible evidence of danger to the child exists. Situations where the court may step in include cases of substance abuse, domestic violence, or a parent who has a history of abuse or neglect.

When a parent violates a visitation order, the other parent can request that the court enforce it by holding the non-compliant parent in contempt.

NOTE: Child support and visitation are two separate matters. A parent cannot withhold visitation if the other does not pay support. Nor can a parent withhold child support if the other parent withholds visitation.

Modification of Visitation Orders

You can modify visitation orders if you or the other parent experiences a substantial change in circumstances that affects the child's welfare. Common reasons for modification include:

- A parent must relocate
- Changes in the child's needs or preferences
- Evidence of abuse or neglect
- Parental non-compliance with existing orders

Either parent can petition the court for a modification of the custody order. The court will decide whether to grant it based on the child's best interests.

We recommend seeking the advice and guidance of an attorney when asking for a modification of visitation or child support orders.

Grandparent and Third-Party Visitation

Grandparents, siblings and other relatives can ask the court for visitation if certain circumstances exist, such as the death of a parent or if the petitioning party had close involvement with the child. Courts only grant grandparent or third-party visitation when it is in the child's best interests and does not interfere with parental rights.

Because grandparents often play a vital role in the lives of their grandchildren, including providing emotional support, stability, and family continuity, the court may allow them visitation rights if divorce, separation, or other circumstances arise when access to the child becomes limited or is denied by one or both parents.

Legal Rights of Grandparents

Each state has its own laws for grandparent visitation. While all 50 states have statutes that allow grandparent visitation, the conditions and likelihood of success differ.

Some states have restrictive visitation statutes[xv] that permit grandparents to seek visitation under specific circumstances, such as when parents divorce, separate, or when one or both parents are deceased. Other states have permissive visitation statutes, which allow grandparents to request visitation in more circumstances, including when the parents are still married, if it is in the child's best interests.

Grandparents do not have automatic rights to visitation. Courts balance the grandparents' requests with the parents' fundamental constitutional right to make decisions about their child's upbringing. In *Troxel v. Granville*[xvi], the U.S. Supreme Court ruled that parental decisions generally take precedence unless denying visitation would harm the child.

CHAPTER 12: PARENTING PLANS

Parenting Plans

A parenting plan is one of the foundational documents in a family law case. It provides a clear roadmap for how divorced or separated parents will share the rights and responsibilities of raising their children.

A well-drafted parenting plan prioritizes the child's best interests, reduces conflict and fosters stability during a time of significant family transition. Courts often require a parenting plan as part of custody proceedings, and once approved, the plan becomes a legally binding agreement that guides co-parenting arrangements.

What is a Parenting Plan?

In most states, divorcing or separating parents must create a parenting plan—a written agreement that outlines each parent's rights, responsibilities and expectations regarding their child's upbringing after separation or divorce.

The plan addresses day-to-day routines and major life decisions, ensuring both parents remain actively involved in their child's life. If the parents cannot agree on a parenting plan, the court will create one based on the child's best interests.

Creating an Effective Parenting Plan

Due to the comprehensive nature of a parenting plan, it takes time to craft one that is in the best interests of the child and reduces disputes between the parents, even when the parents communicate or are able to agree on all matters. This isn't a document you want to leave until the last minute. Tips for creating a parenting plan that is in the best interests of the child and that will make co-parenting less stressful include:

- **Start Early**: Begin negotiating the parenting plan as soon as possible. Early, collaborative planning helps reduce conflict and ensures the plan reflects both parents' input while meeting the child's needs.

- **One Section at a Time and Cooperate**: The amount of information in a parenting plan may be overwhelming for some. Work on one section at a time until you can reach an agreement. If you cannot agree after a few hours or a day of discussions on that section, move on to the next session. You can always return to sections you do not agree with.

- **Focus on the Child's Best Interests**: Always prioritize the child's best interests when creating a parenting plan. Consider the child's age, developmental stage, school schedule and emotional needs at every step.

- **Be Detailed and Specific**: Even if you get along and do not think you need all of the details, you never know what will happen in the future. Be detailed and specific with every entry in your child's parenting plan. Clearly outline schedules, responsibilities and procedures for decision-making and dispute resolutions.

- **Remain Flexible**: Although structure is important, life changes, such as health issues, job shifts and the child's evolving needs, require flexibility. Build mechanisms for making temporary or permanent changes to the plan.

- **Consult Legal Professionals**: A family law attorney can guide you through the process of creating a parenting plan that is in the best interests of the child. The attorney can also guide you in circumstances where your spouse does not agree. Because the attorney doesn't have an emotional attachment to the parenting plan, he or she can let you know if either your or your spouse's requests are irrational.

How a Parenting Plan Can Make Determining Custody Arrangements Smoother

When you create a comprehensive parenting plan, it supports smoother custody arrangements in several key ways, including:

Reduces Conflict and Misunderstandings

When you clearly outline each parent's responsibilities, schedules and expectations in the parenting plan, you can minimize ambiguity and potential disputes. Clarity helps prevent misunderstandings regarding custody, visitation and decision-making, which are common sources of post-divorce conflict.

Promotes Stability and Consistency for Children

A detailed parenting plan establishes predictable routines and consistent rules across both households, giving children the stability they need to adjust to new family dynamics. They are also able to maintain a sense of security during and after the transition and know what each parent expects of them.

Facilitates Effective Communication

Comprehensive parenting plans include guidelines dictating how parents should communicate about the child's needs and important matters. This structure fosters open, respectful, and timely communication, which is essential for effective co-parenting.

Address All Key Issues Upfront

By covering custody, visitation schedules, decision-making authority, financial responsibilities and dispute resolution in a parenting plan, you address potential issues before they arise, which makes day-to-day co-parenting smoother.

Encourages Cooperative Co-Parenting

A comprehensive parenting plan fosters co-parenting by clearly defining the roles and responsibilities of both parents. They are more likely to work together in a constructive manner, which benefits the child and can strengthen parent-child relationships.

Provides a Framework for Conflict Resolution

When you include procedures for handling disagreements, such as mediation or arbitration, it helps parents resolve issues efficiently without having to return to court. It also reduces stress for everyone involved.

Protects the Child's Best Interests

A comprehensive parenting plan protects the child's best interests by ensuring that the parents remain focused on the child's emotional, physical and developmental needs instead of what the parents want (which may not be in the best interests of the child).

Allows for Flexibility and Adaptations

A well-crafted parenting plan includes provisions for reviewing and modifying arrangements as the child's needs or family circumstances change, which supports the long-term success of the parenting plan and co-parenting.

Establishes Legal Accountability

Once the court approves the parenting plan, it becomes legally binding, providing a mechanism for enforcement if one parent does not comply. The complying parent can try to mediate the situation or ask the court to compel the non-compliant parent to obey the parenting plan. If that fails, the complying parent can ask the court to hold the non-compliant parent in contempt. The non-compliant parent would face penalties as allowed by state law.

Reduces Stress for Parents and Children

A comprehensive parenting plan also reduces stress for the parents and the children by providing a clear, predictable structure and minimizing uncertainty. The plan also supports healthier post-divorce family relationships.

Key Components of a Parenting Plan

The more comprehensive the parenting plan, the less likely you are to have disputes between the parents. A comprehensive parenting plan should address the following elements to minimize ambiguity and future disputes:

- **Custody and Residential Schedule**: This section specifies where the child will live and when, including regular weekdays, weekends, holidays, birthdays and school vacations. Include pick-up and drop-off times, locations and procedures for transitions between households.

- **Decision-Making Responsibilities**: Define how each parent will make major decisions about education, healthcare, religion and extracurricular activities. State whether the decision-making is joint or sole, and outline procedures for resolving disagreements.

- **Parenting Time (Visitation)**: This section outlines the schedule for the non-residential parent, including pickup and drop-off times and locations, as well as arrangements for special occasions and holidays. Include contingency plans for emergencies or unforeseen circumstances. Also, include a section giving each parent the right of first refusal when a parent needs a sitter.

- **Communication Guidelines**: Outline how parents will communicate with each other, whether by email, phone or a parenting app. Include rules for communicating with the child during the other parent's parenting time, e.g., phone, email, video calls, and texts. Include expectations for timely responses.

- **Information Sharing**: List protocols for sharing important information about the child's health, education and welfare.

- **Transportation and Exchanges**: Specify how and where you will exchange the child, taking into account safety and convenience. Include rules for out-of-state and international travel, notice requirements, permissions and the handling of passports.

- **Financial Responsibilities**: This section addresses child support, health insurance, uncovered medical expenses, extracurricular activities, and other costs not covered by standard support orders. Include payment schedules or timeframes.

- **Modification and Review**: Include procedures and timeframes for reviewing and updating the parenting plan as the child's needs or family circumstances change. Include the method of discussion, whether in-person, via email, over the phone, or through your attorneys.

- **Medical and Healthcare Arrangements**: Include guidelines for making medical decisions, sharing medical information and handling emergencies. Include topics such as vaccinations, access to records, notification requirements, preferred hospital for emergencies, and the child's medical providers.

- **Education and Schooling**: Specify who is responsible for school enrollment, attendance at parent-teacher conferences and decisions about tutoring or special education services.

- **Child's Belongings and Personal Items**: Clarify how you will manage the child's clothing, school supplies and personal items between households.

- **Special Considerations**: Account for unique needs, such as medical conditions, educational plans, travel restrictions, and/or concerns related to domestic violence.

- **Right of First Refusal**: Include a clause stating that if a parent cannot care for the child during his or her scheduled time, the other parent has the first opportunity to provide care prior to selecting a third party.

- **Relocation Provisions**: Address what happens if a parent wishes to or must move, including required notice, limitations on relocation, and procedures for modifying the plan if relocation affects the child's schedule or relationship with either parent.

- **Dispute Resolution Procedures**: Outline steps for resolving conflicts, such as mediation, prior to returning to court. This helps the parties to prevent escalation and encourages cooperative problem-solving.

- **Enforcement and Consequences**: State the consequences for failing to follow the plan, including the use of mediation or seeking court enforcement.

Special Considerations

Part of a well-constructed parenting plan includes special considerations for events that may have already occurred or may not have yet happened. For example, you may not plan on long-distance parenting, but one spouse may need to move out of state to remain employed.

When you plan ahead for these considerations—or include them if they have happened or are currently happening—you can also avoid contention and stress.

Some special considerations may include:

- **Long-Distance Parenting**: Include travel arrangements and new custody and visitation schedules should one of the parents' employers request the parent to relocate or should the parent decide to relocate voluntarily.
- **Domestic Violence**: If the family has a history of abuse or neglect, the plan should prioritize safety, possibly including supervised visitation (more on visitation below) or safe exchange locations.
  - **Blended Families and Remarriage**: You may need to adjust the parenting plan to accommodate new family members or changing household dynamics. While it may be difficult to create a new plan before you start a new relationship, you can add rules as to when the parenting plan should change, including limiting changes that would not benefit the other spouse or that would be against the best interests of the child.

CHAPTER 13: PARENTING CLASSES

Divorce is not only life-changing for parents but also for children. Because of the unique stresses and adjustments families face during the transition to living separately, many courts require divorcing parents to participate in parenting classes.

These classes provide parents with the knowledge, skills and support necessary to navigate co-parenting with the child's best interests at heart. They help divorcing couples focus on the impact of divorce on children, develop effective communication and conflict resolution skills, and foster a cooperative co-parenting relationship.

Parenting classes[xvii] typically cover topics such as the emotional and behavioral effects of divorce on children, age-appropriate parenting strategies, managing stress, and the importance of maintaining a positive, stable environment for children.

Some programs also address legal responsibilities, offer guidance on creating parenting plans and provide tools for minimizing conflict and promoting healthy adjustments for all family members.

Depending on your state's laws, participation may be in-person or online. Once you complete the parenting class, you should receive a certificate to file with the court for proof of taking the parenting class.

States With Mandatory Parenting Class Statutes

Some states require divorcing parents to take parenting classes, while others have mandatory requirements in certain counties. Other states do not require a parenting class, though we recommend taking one.

> **These states require mandatory parenting classes at the time of printing. Check with an attorney or the court to see if your state or the county where you filed for divorce requires parents to take a parenting course or seminar.**

Florida

Florida's Department of Children and Families approves parenting courses. The courses must be a minimum of four hours. The Parent Education and Family Stabilization Course includes several topics, including:

- The legal aspects of deciding child-related issues between parents.
- The emotional aspects of separation and divorce on adults and children.
- Family relationships and family dynamics.
- Financial responsibilities to a child.
- Issues regarding spousal or child abuse and neglect, and a list of agencies that provide assistance with these issues.
- Skill-based relationship education related to parenting, workplace, school, neighborhood and civic relationships.
- The needs of children who have identified special needs or emotional concerns.

The Department of Children and Families must approve any institution offering parenting courses. You can obtain a list of parenting courses and their locations through the family court in the county where you filed the divorce.

For dissolution actions, the parties must take the course within 45 days of filing the Petition for Dissolution of Marriage.

Courts can hold individuals who fail to attend the required parenting course in contempt and may deny shared parental responsibility or time-sharing (Fla. Stat. § 61.21).

Hawaii

Hawaii requires all divorcing parents to attend the Kids First[xviii] [xix] course. Children aged 6 to 18 are also required to attend.

Idaho

The state of Idaho does not have a parenting class but instead mandates that divorcing couples take "Focus on Children[xx]," a course designed to provide separated or divorced parents with potential tools to communicate effectively on parenting issues while removing children from parental conflict.

The course is offered via an online video that you may view independently. It takes about 1.5 to 2 hours to watch the video and complete the required questionnaire.

The courts order everyone to take the course if they have children under the age of 18.

Illinois

Divorcing parties and those involved in a post-judgment proceeding who have minor children must attend an educational program concerning the effects of divorce on the children (750 ILCS 50/404.1).

Massachusetts

"Two Families Now[xxi]" is the co-parenting education course required by the court for unmarried and married parents appearing before the Probate and Family Court. It is a 4-hour online course that parents can take at their own pace. Parents can take the course on a computer, tablet, or smartphone.

If you file a Complaint for Divorce, a Complaint for Separate Support, a Complaint to Establish Paternity or a Complaint for Custody/Support/Parenting Time, you must take the course.

Parents have 30 calendar days from the date the complaint is served to register for the online course and 30 days from the date of registration to complete the course. Each parent must file the Certificate of Completion with the court within 14 calendar days of the completion date. The court may impose sanctions for failing to complete the co-parenting course.

Michigan

While Michigan does not have a statute that mandates parents to take a parenting course, many courts require parents to attend the SMILE program[xxii].

Minnesota

Parents of minor children must take a course that educates them about the impact that divorce, family restructuring, and judicial proceedings have on children and families. The course also covers methods for preventing parenting time conflicts and educates parents about dispute resolution options.

Attendance is mandatory, and the course is a minimum of 8 hours. Courts may also order those involved in other proceedings, including custody, support, or parenting time actions, to attend the parent education program. Parents must begin the course within 30 days after the first filing with the court.

The program notifies the court of any person who fails to attend the course as ordered by the court. The court may impose sanctions on those who do not attend or complete the parent education program (Minn. Stat. §518-157).

Missouri

Parents divorcing or involved in post-judgment proceedings involving custody or child support must attend an education course that covers the effects of the dissolution of marriage on minor children. It also covers the benefits of alternative dispute resolution, including mediation (Mo. Rev. Stat. §452.600).

Nebraska

All parties going through a divorce are required to attend a basic-level parenting education course. If the couple has a history of domestic violence, child abuse or neglect, or unresolved parental conflict, the court may order the parties to attend a second-level parenting education course after completing the basic-level parenting education course.

The course covers information on the developmental stages of the children, adjustment of a child to parental separation, the litigation and court processes, conflict management, alternative dispute resolution, guidelines for parenting time and visitation, stress reduction, safety and transition plans, and information about children and parents affected by child abuse, unresolved parental conflict or intimate partner abuse (Neb. Rev. Stat. §43-2928).

New Hampshire

Parents of minor children in New Hampshire must attend a seminar conducted by a certified family therapist or another person certified by the family court. The seminar covers the best way to address problems the children face as a result of divorce or separation. It can also cover various divorce options, including arbitration, mediation, and litigation.

The session covers the following:

- Understanding the process of divorce, including the interaction between the parent and child, areas of adjustment and areas of concern.
- How children react to divorce or separation.
- How to spot problems.
- How to tell the children about divorce or separation.
- How to keep communication open.
- How parents can help children during divorce, including offering specific strategies, ideas, tools and resources for assistance.
- How parents can support children after the divorce or separation, new family structures and how to deal with different sets of rules.

The presenter(s) may also discuss domestic violence and communication in those cases (N.H. Rev. Stat. §458-D:3).

New Jersey

The "Parents' Education Program" is mandatory in New Jersey for parents going through divorce. The program helps people going through the divorce process understand divorce, separation and custody.

The courts administer the program, which is available twice a month. Factors covered in the program include:

- The legal process and cost of divorce or separation, including arbitration and mediation.

- Financial responsibilities for the children.
- Interaction between the parent and child, the family relationship and areas of adjustment and concern during the divorce or separation process.
- Children's reactions to divorce or separation, spotting problems, what to tell the children about divorce or separation, keeping communication open and how to answer questions and concerns the children may have about the divorce or separation process.
- How parents can support their children during the divorce or separation, specific strategies, ideas, tools, and resources for assistance.
- How parents can help children cope after divorce or separation, and how to navigate new family structures and different sets of rules.

The course also covers instances when cooperation may be inappropriate due to domestic violence (N.J. Stat. §2A:34-12.3).

Oklahoma

Anyone going through an action for divorce, separate maintenance, guardianship, paternity, custody or visitation, including modifications or enforcement of a court order, who has children under the age of 18, must attend an educational program regarding the impact of co-parenting during and after the action.

The course also covers the implications for visitation and conflict management, the development of children, separate financial responsibility for children and other topics as determined by the court.

Specific topics may include:

- Short and long-term effects of divorce on the child's well-being.
- Reconciliation as an optional outcome.
- Effects of family violence.
- Potential behaviors exhibited by children.
- The child's emotional state during and after divorce, and how to respond to the child's needs.

- Communication strategies to reduce conflict and facilitate cooperative co-parenting.
- Area resources to address substance abuse or other addictions, family violence, behavioral health, financial planning and individual couples counseling.

The program administrator will issue a certificate of completion that you or your attorney must file with the court. Parents must complete the course within 45 days of receiving a temporary order. The court will not issue a final disposition of child custody until the parties complete the course (Okla. Stat. tit. 43, §107.2).

Tennessee

Every parent going through a divorce in Tennessee is required to attend a parent education seminar as soon as possible after filing the complaint. The seminar must be at least four hours in duration, and the minor children cannot attend. It must include:

- A 30-minute video on adverse childhood experiences.
- A discussion on alternative dispute resolution.
- Marriage counseling.
- Common perpetrator attitudes and conduct in domestic violence.
- The judicial process (Tenn. Code Ann. §36-6-408).

Virginia

Parties with minor children who file a contested petition for custody, visitation or support must show proof of attending the educational seminar within 12 months prior to their court appearance or that they shall attend the seminar within 45 days thereafter.

The parties generally do not have to attend the seminar if their case is uncontested unless the court requests it based on good cause.

The seminar is a minimum of four hours and covers the effects of separation or divorce on children, parenting responsibilities, options for conflict resolution and financial responsibilities (Va. Code Ann. §16.1-278.15).

West Virginia

Parties to an action for divorce, paternity, support, separate maintenance or custody proceedings must attend parent education classes to learn of the effects of divorce and custody disputes on their children. The course also teaches parents ways to help their children and minimize trauma (W. Va. Code §48-9-104).

Wisconsin

Parties to an action affecting the family, such as divorce or custody, who have minor children, are required to attend a parent education course. The course is four hours or less. If a party refuses to attend or attends and does not pay, the court can hold that party in contempt.

The class may address issues such as child development, the impact of parental separation on a child's development, family dynamics, and strategies that parents can use to reduce their child's stress during and after divorce or separation (Wis. Stat. §767.401).

CHAPTER 14: PARENTAL ALIENATION

Parental alienation[xxiii], sometimes referred to as child alienation, is when a parent or another person—usually one of the parents or a grandparent—deliberately and without legitimate justification undermines and/or damages a child's relationship with the other parent. It generally involves manipulation, negative comments or actions intended to isolate the child from the targeted parent.

The alienating parent may not fully realize his or her behavior is affecting the child's relationship with the targeted parent, although in most cases, the alienation is intentional.

A parent involved in alienating the child from the other parent, whether intentionally or unconsciously, harms the child's emotional and psychological well-being in addition to damaging the child's relationship with the other parent.

Children affected can experience confusion, anxiety, loyalty conflicts, depression and long-term difficulty forming healthy relationships. Because the child loses the opportunity for a meaningful relationship with the alienated parent, the damage is profound. It can even affect extended family members, even if the alienating parent does not specifically target them.

Court Intervention and Remedies

The courts take allegations of parental alienation seriously, especially when the alienating parent's conduct is intentionally undermining the child's relationship with the other parent. If the affected parent can prove alienation, courts may intervene by:

- Requiring family or reunification counseling to repair the parent-child relationship and address underlying issues.
- Modify custody agreements, even awarding primary or sole custody to the alienated parent if it is in the child's best interests and necessary to stop the alienating behavior by the other parent.
- Imposing sanctions and requiring parenting classes.
- Setting strict guidelines for parental conduct and communication to prevent further alienation.

It is imperative that the alienated parent distinguish parental alienation from justified estrangement, where the child's reluctance to see a parent is because of the parent's substance abuse, neglect or other legitimate concerns.

If the case is an actual case of alienation, the child's rejection is disproportionate to any behavior by the alienating parent.

If you suspect the other parent is engaging in alienating behavior, contact an experienced family law attorney as soon as possible.

CHAPTER 15: CHILDREN TESTIFYING IN DIVORCE COURT

Sometimes, the court will ask a child to testify in a divorce or custody case. The court will take measures to protect the children from emotional harm and unnecessary trauma[xxiv]. In most cases, courts limit a child's direct involvement in proceedings and prefer to use alternative methods to gather the child's input.

Handling a Child's Testimony

The court takes several factors into consideration prior to asking the child to testify, including the child's age, maturity level and his or her ability to understand lies. The court also ensures the child is competent to testify, e.g., by ensuring the child can communicate clearly and appreciate the importance of telling the truth.

Most states' laws do not provide a strict age limit for children testifying, but age is a key factor. Courts very rarely call young children to testify. However, if they are young, the courts handle the process with extra caution to avoid undue stress.

The courts may use less adversarial settings, such as *in camera* interviews, which are private conversations between the judge and the child in the judge's chambers, or they may appoint a professional to represent the child's interests.

Common alternatives include:

- Appointing a guardian *ad litem*—a special advocate to investigate and represent the child's best interests.
- Ordering custody evaluators or child psychologists to assess the child's needs and family dynamics. These professionals then provide their recommendations to the court.
- *In camera* interviews.

The court may consider the child's wishes regarding custody or visitation, especially if the child is older and has sufficient maturity. However, his or her preference is one of many factors courts use and is not determinative.

Limiting Trauma for a Child Testifying in a Divorce or Custody Case

The last thing the court wants to do is to place the child in the middle of parental disputes or expose them to unnecessary emotional distress. Courts only ask a child to testify if his or her input is essential to resolving the custody or safety issues.

When the court must ask for a child's testimony, it minimizes the emotional impact through careful questioning, supportive environments and the involvement of trained professionals.

CHAPTER 16: GUARDIANS *AD LITEM*

In some family law cases, a child needs someone to look out for his or her best interests. This person is known as a Guardian *ad Litem* (GAL). The court appoints a GAL to represent and protect the best interests of the child or a legally incapacitated person (ward) during court proceedings.

The most common court cases that use a Guardian *ad Litem* are in family law cases involving disputes over child custody, allegations of neglect and/or abuse, adoption cases or when a party is unable to represent his or her own interests adequately due to incapacity.

The Guardian *ad Litem* acts as the court's factfinder and may conduct investigations, interview relevant parties, review documents and make recommendations to the court regarding outcomes that serve the child's welfare.

State and local laws govern GALs, although their training, qualifications and duties may vary. In some jurisdictions, the GAL must be an attorney, while in others, the GAL can be a non-lawyer with specialized training. Some states even allow volunteers to work under supervision.

The GAL must have training in child development, the dynamics of abuse and neglect, and must know the legal standards for determining a child's best interests.

Guardian *ad Litem* vs. Traditional Guardian or Conservator

The Guardian *ad Litem* only takes responsibility for his or her ward during the pendency of a case, whereas a traditional guardian's or conservator's responsibility over their ward is ongoing. Additionally, a traditional guardian or conservator has responsibility over the ward's ongoing personal and financial issues.

A GAL does not assume custody or ongoing guardianship of the ward—the law limits it to the case at hand only. The GAL also does not have authority over the ward's life outside of the legal matter for which the court appointed him or her. Once the case ends, the GAL's responsibility ends.

State and Federal Statutes

Each state has its own statutes governing a Guardian *ad Litem*. However, the Child Abuse Prevention and Treatment Act, a federal law, dictates that states must appoint trained GALs for children in abuse or neglect proceedings as a condition for federal funding.

The Role of the Guardian *ad Litem* in Court Proceedings

The Guardian *ad Litem* plays a significant role in family law cases, especially those involving the welfare of children. Their responsibilities ensure the court receives a thorough, impartial and child-centered perspective.

The GAL's first duty is to conduct a comprehensive investigation into the circumstances of the case, including:

- Interviewing key individuals, including the child, parents, caregivers and other relevant people, including counselors, teachers, advocates and medical professionals. These interviews help the GAL understand family dynamics, the child's needs and concerns about safety and well-being.
- Reviewing records, including medical, psychological and educational records to assess the child's health, history of trauma, academic progress and any special needs the child may have.
- Observing interactions between the child and others at home, school and during supervised visits to gain more insight into the child's environment and relationships.

After completing the investigation, the GAL presents his or her findings to the court or may advocate in court for the child's best interests. GALs who advocate for the minor child present legal arguments in court.

Regardless of how the GAL disseminates the information to the court, he or she participates in the legal process. A GAL attends hearings, files motions and other court documents, cross-examines witnesses and more.

CHAPTER 17: CHILD SUPPORT

Child support ensures that children receive the financial support they require once their parents separate or divorce. Many people believe that child support is unfair—that it is too high. However, child support is **not** at the discretion of the court. Every state has a formula, as dictated in its statutes, for determining the amount of support each parent pays. Only three states—Texas[xxv], Mississippi[xxvi] and North Dakota[xxvii]—base child support on one parent's income.

Mississippi bases child support on the non-custodial parent's adjusted gross income, while North Dakota and Texas base child support on the non-custodial parent's net income.

Legal Foundations of Child Support

Every child, regardless of their state of residence, has the right to financial support from both parents, irrespective of their marital status. Biological and adoptive parents must contribute to their child's care, welfare, nurture, support and education until the child reaches the age of majority or graduates from high school—generally, whichever comes later.

The custodial parent typically receives child support from the non-custodial parent. In some cases, when neither parent has custody, the court may require both parents to pay support to a third-party custodian.

What Child Support Covers

Child support covers the child's basic needs, including:

- Housing
- Food
- Clothing
- Health insurance and uncovered medical expenses
- Childcare expenses
- Daycare expenses

In certain states, child support does not cover extracurricular activities and special expenses and may require an additional agreement between the parents. Child support does not cover private school tuition; however, parents can include the cost in the childcare box if they wish to factor it into the formula.

Some parents agree that the parent who wishes the child to attend private school pays for the full tuition if the other parent prefers the child to attend public school.

Calculating Child Support

Every state has guidelines, which are periodically updated. Most states use the income shares model, which considers both parties' incomes and divides the support obligation proportionally.

The guidelines use each parent's gross income from all sources and the number of children common to the parties. It also adjusts the amount based on the amount of time the children spend with each parent. Support guidelines require you to add childcare, daycare expenses, health insurance, and recurring medical costs above the base amount due.

The guidelines also consider support obligations to other children from different relationships. Additionally, the court may adjust the guideline amount if a parent has special circumstances, such as high medical expenses or differences in parenting time.

States use one of three models to calculate child support: The income shares model, which is the most common; the percentage of income model; and the Melson formula.

Income Shares Model

The income shares model subscribes to the theory that a child should receive the same proportion of parental income that he or she would receive if the parents were to live together. The guidelines use both parents' incomes to determine the total support obligation, dividing the total in proportion to each parent's income.

Additional factors, such as childcare expenses, health insurance and uncovered medical costs, also follow the same formula.

Alabama	Arizona	Arkansas	California	Colorado
Connecticut	Florida	Georgia	Idaho	Illinois
Indiana	Iowa	Kansas	Kentucky	Louisiana
Maine	Maryland	Massachusetts	Michigan	Minnesota
Missouri	Nebraska	New Hampshire	New Jersey	New Mexico
New York	North Carolina	Ohio	Oklahoma	Oregon
Pennsylvania	Rhode Island	South Carolina	South Dakota	Tennessee
Utah	Vermont	Virginia	Washington	West Virginia
Wyoming				

Figure 1: States Using the Income Shares Model

How to Calculate Child Support Using the Income Shares Model

Check the guidelines to determine whether to start with gross, adjusted gross or net monthly income. If the guidelines begin with gross monthly income, follow the instructions on the child support guidelines form to determine whether you figure adjusted gross or net monthly income.

The example we are using (Florida) uses net monthly income, but the steps are essentially the same for most states using the income shares model, regardless of whether it is based on net monthly income or not.

If you are following along with the Florida child support guidelines, note that the steps below and line numbers may not match, as we've broken down the form's steps to make it easier to follow for other states that may have a slightly different process.

Figure the Base Amount Due

STEP 1: Enter the parents' net monthly income in the appropriate column, titled "Petitioner" and "Respondent" or "Mother" and "Father."

STEP 2: Enter the total. For example, if the petitioner takes home $4,000 and the respondent takes home $3,000, the total would be $7,000.

STEP 3: Enter the number of children common to the parties.

STEP 4: Refer to the child support guidelines instructions to find the base amount. In this example, the parties have one child, and the base amount from the child support guidelines chart is $1,212. Enter that amount in the appropriate box.

STEP 5: Find the percentage of financial responsibility for the petitioner by dividing his or her net income by the parties' total net income (4000/7000) for a result of 57 percent. Enter that number in the appropriate column.

STEP 6: Find the percentage of financial responsibility for the respondent by dividing his or her net income by the parties' total net income (3000/7000) for a result of 43 percent. Enter that number in the appropriate column.

STEP 7: Determine the share of basic monthly income by multiplying the basic total amount ($1,212) by the percentage for each parent. Enter the amount in the appropriate column. This amount is the base amount of child support due from each parent. In this example, the amounts are $690.84 for the petitioner and $521.16 for the respondent.

Calculate Additional Costs

STEP 8: Enter the total monthly childcare costs. In this example, it is $400.

STEP 9: Enter the total monthly premiums for the child's portion of your healthcare insurance policy. Do not enter the full premiums, as that includes healthcare for the parents. In this example, it is $50.

STEP 10: Enter the total monthly uncovered medical, dental and prescription medication costs per month. This amount should be an average. To determine the average monthly costs, add all uncovered medical expenses for the child from January 1 to December 31 of the previous year and then divide that amount by 12. Enter that amount in the box for uncovered health care. Do not enter insurance premiums. In this example, it is $50.

STEP 11: Add the total childcare, health insurance premiums and uncovered medical expenses and enter that number on the appropriate line. In this example, it is $500.

STEP 12: Multiply the total from Step 10 by the percentages from Steps 4 and 5. Enter the result from using the percentage in Step 4 in the petitioner's column and the result from using the percentage in Step 5 in the respondent's column. In this example, the results are 500 divided by 57 percent for the petitioner, for a result of $285, and 500 divided by 43 percent for the respondent, for a result of $215.

STEP 13: Enter the monthly childcare payments actually made. If the payments are $400 and the respondent pays the full amount, enter $400 in the respondent's column.

STEP 14: Enter the monthly health insurance payments actually made. In this example, the petitioner pays $50 per month in health insurance premiums. Enter the amount in the petitioner's column.

STEP 15: Enter payments for uncovered healthcare. Use the average amount by adding all of the payments made by the parties over the previous year and dividing them by 12. If only one parent made payments, enter that amount in his or her column. If both parents made payments for uncovered medical expenses, add the father's for the year and then the mother's for the year. Divide each number by 12 and enter it in the appropriate column. In this example, only the respondent paid the average of $50 per month, so enter that amount in the respondent's column.

STEP 16: Add the total of payments made by each parent. In this case, the petitioner paid $50 and the respondent paid $450.

STEP 17: Figure the minimum child support obligations for each parent by adding the amounts in Steps 6 and 11 and subtracting the amount in Step 15. In this example, the petitioner's minimum child support obligation is $925.84, and the respondent's minimum basic child support obligation is $286.16.

Stop here if you have a regular visitation schedule. If each parent has at least 73 overnights per year, then continue with the Gross-Up Method.

Depending on your state, the child support guidelines may use a similar method or another method to determine the adjustment in child support for the change in custody and/or visitation.

Determine Child Support Using the Gross-Up Method

STEP 18: Multiply the basic monthly obligation from Step 3 by 150 percent ($1,212 x 1.5). In this example, the amount is $1,818.

STEP 19: Multiply the number from Step 17 by each party's percentage. In this example, the petitioner's amount is 57 percent times 1818, resulting in $1,036.26. The respondent's result is 43 percent times 1818, resulting in $781.74.

STEP 20: Count the number of overnights the children spend with each parent. Enter those amounts on the child support guidelines worksheet in the appropriate column or box. In our example, the children spend 181 nights with the petitioner and 182 nights with the respondent.

STEP 21: Multiply each number by 100 and then divide the sum by 365. In this example, the petitioner spends 181 nights with the children, resulting in 181 x 100 = 18,100 divided by 365, which equals 49.59 percent. The respondent spends 182 nights with the children, resulting in 182 x 100 = 18,200 divided by 365, which equals 49.86 percent. Enter the results in the appropriate column.

STEP 22: Multiply the petitioner's support by the respondent's number of overnights (1036.26 x .4986) for a result of $516.67.

STEP 23: Multiply the respondent's support by the petitioner's number of overnights (781.74 x .4959) for a result of $387.66.

STEP 24: Calculate additional support for childcare, health insurance and uncovered medical expenses. Enter the original numbers in the total column. They will total $500, as they did in Step 10.

STEP 25: Multiply the number from Step 23 ($500) by the percentage from Steps 4 and 5 (for each parent). In this example, the amount for the petitioner is $285, and the amount for the respondent is $215.

STEP 26: Enter the amount of childcare actually paid. In this example, the respondent pays $400 per month, so enter that amount in the respondent's column.

STEP 27: Enter the amount of monthly health insurance payments actually made. In this example, the petitioner pays $50 per month, so enter that amount in the petitioner's column.

STEP 28: Enter the amount of uncovered medical expenses actually incurred. In this example, the respondent pays an average of $50 per month, so enter that amount in the respondent's column.

STEP 29: Add the two columns. The petitioner pays $50 for additional expenses each month, while the respondent pays $450 per month for additional expenses.

STEP 30: Subtract the amount in Step 28 from the amount in Step 24. In this example, the result for the petitioner is 285 minus 50, for a result of $235. Enter this number in the petitioner's column. The result for the respondent is 215 minus 450, which results in a negative number, so enter zero in the respondent's column.

STEP 31: Calculate the total child support owed from the petitioner to the respondent by adding the amount in Step 21 ($516.67) and the amount for the petitioner in Step 29 ($235) for a total of $751.67.

STEP 32: Calculate the total child support owed from the respondent to the petitioner by adding the amount in Step 22 ($387.66) to the amount for the respondent in Step 29 (0), for a total of $387.66.

STEP 33: Calculate the presumptive child support by comparing the amounts from Steps 30 and 31. Subtract the smaller amount from the larger amount owed and enter the number in the column for the parent that owes the larger amount. In this example, the petitioner owes $751.67 and has the larger amount. Subtract the amount in Step 31 (387.66) for a balance of $364.01 due from the petitioner to the respondent. The petitioner pays the respondent $364.01.

Fixed Percentage of Income Model

This method of calculating child support assigns a set percentage of the non-custodial parent's income to child support. It does not consider other factors. This method is not as fair as the income shares method, and only a few states use it.

Depending on the state, it may use the flat percentage method, in which the same percentage of income applies regardless of income level, or the varying percentage method, in which the percentage changes based on the income bracket of the number of children.

Alaska Child Support Calculations

Alaska uses several calculations to determine child support, including base income, the type of custody and the number of children[xxviii].

STEP 1: Calculate the adjusted annual income for each parent and enter it in the appropriate column.

STEP 2: Multiply the adjusted annual income by one of the following percentages for each parent:

- .20 for one child
- .27 for two children
- .33 for three children

Add .03 for each additional child. For example, if you have four children, the percentage is .36. Enter the amount in the appropriate column for each parent. If this amount is $600 or less, enter $600 in the box for Annual Child Support.

STEP 3: Enter the date payments start and the date they are due every month.

STEP 4: Choose the type of custody, whether primary, shared, divided or hybrid.

Primary Custody: If the child stays with one parent more than 70 percent of the overnights (256), complete the calculation for primary custody by dividing the Annual Child Support Amount *of the parent who has fewer overnights* by 12. Tick the box for Party A or Party B.

Shared Custody: The children stay with each parent at least 30 percent of the overnights (110 or more each parent). Enter the child support payment determined on Line 10 of Form DR-306.

Divided Custody: Each parent has primary custody of one or more children of the marriage. Enter the child support payment from Section 6 of DR-307.

Hybrid Custody: The parents share custody of at least one child, and one or both parents have primary custody of a child or children from a previous marriage. Enter the amount for hybrid custody in the appropriate column.

STEP 5: Determine the amount for the child's health insurance coverage if the Indian Health Service or Tricare does not cover the child. Answer the four questions regarding health insurance.

STEP 6: If the responses to Questions 3 and 4 are 'No,' one of the parents must agree to provide insurance, provided it is available at a reasonable cost. Check the box for the providing party and enter the cost of the monthly premiums. Tick the appropriate boxes to indicate where the parent obtained the insurance. Health insurance is typically paid equally by both parties, with the other party's share deducted from the child support amount. Be sure to list *only* the cost of the child's portion of health insurance.

STEP 7: Complete the section regarding the child's uncovered healthcare expenses.

STEP 8: Enter the monthly child support payment from Step 4 on Line 5a.

STEP 9: Enter half of the insurance payment from Step 6 on Line 5b.

STEP 10: Enter half of the uncovered medical expenses on Line 5c.

STEP 11: Add lines 5a through 5c and enter that amount on Line 5d.

STEP 12: Tick the appropriate box in Section 6 based on your annual income.

STEP 13: Complete Sections 7 and 8 for seasonal income and travel expenses.

STEP 14: Sign the bottom of both pages. This form is part of the Petition for Dissolution of Marriage with Children (DR-105). The court will determine child support based on your answers.

Mississippi Child Support Calculations

Mississippi determines child support based on the adjusted gross income[xxix] of the non-custodial parent.

Number of Children	Percentage of Gross Income
1	14%
2	20%
3	22%
4	24%

Figure 2: Mississippi Percentages per Child Based on Adjusted Gross Income

Wisconsin Child Support Guidelines

The state of Wisconsin provides several formulas for determining child support[xxx]:

- **Shared Placement Cases**: When the parties each have the children at least 25 percent of the year (92 or more days spent with each parent).

- **Serial Family Cases**: If a parent has children from another relationship, the court may adjust the parent's income for later child support cases.

- **Split Placement Cases**: When a family has two or more children and at least one of the children stays with each parent, but not all of the children, Wisconsin can prorate the child support standard.

  Cases with two children: 12.5 percent of income for each child.

  Cases with three children: 9.67 percent of income for each child.

  Cases with four children: 7.75 percent of income for each child.

  Cases with five children: 6.8 percent of income for each child.

Child Support Standard Designated Percentage

The Child Support Guidelines apply the following percentages to the parents' income for child support.

- **1 Child**: 17 percent
- **2 Children**: 25 percent
- **3 Children**: 29 percent
- **4 Children**: 31 percent
- **5 Children**: 34 percent

High-Income Payer Cases

If the paying parent's income exceeds $84,000 per year[xxxi], the court may apply the high-income payer guidelines. The Child Support Standard applies to the first $83,999.99 in income. A second set of guidelines applies to income between $84,000 and $150,000 per year. A third set of guidelines applies to any income over $150,000.

The guidelines for the first $7,000/month of income are:

- 17% of income for 1 child
- 25% of income for 2 children
- 29% of income for 3 children
- 31% of income for 4 children
- 34% of income for 5 or more children

The guidelines for the portion of income between $7,000/month and $12,500/month ($84,000 - $150,000/year) are:

- 14% of income for 1 child
- 20% of income for 2 children
- 23% of income for 3 children
- 25% of income for 4 children
- 27% of income for 5 or more children

The guidelines for the portion of income that is more than $12,500/month ($150,000/year):

- 10% of income for 1 child
- 15% of income for 2 children
- 17% of income for 3 children
- 19% of income for 4 children
- 20% of income for 5 or more children

Low-Income Cases

If the paying parent's income is less than $1,485 per month, the court may use the low-income payer guidelines[xxxii]. This table changes every year.

Varying Percentage Model for Child Support Calculations

The following states use the varying percentage model for child support calculations.

North Dakota

The percentage varies by income and the number of children[xxxiii] the parents have in common. North Dakota uses a schedule of income and percentages[xxxiv].

Texas

The paying parent pays 20 percent for one child[xxxv], with the rate increasing for each additional child. The state places a cap on the number of children based on specific circumstances.

No. of Children	Standard Income	Low Income*
1	20%	15%
2	25%	20%
3	30%	25%
4	35%	30%
5	40%	35%
6+ Children	Not less than the amount for 5 children	Not less than the amount for 5 children
		* Obligor's monthly net resources less than $1,000

Figure 3: Texas Child Support Percentages

Nevada

In Nevada, the paying parent pays a percentage based on a sliding income scale[xxxvi]. The court has the discretion to lower percentages for low-income obligors.

Example for one child for an obligor who makes $50,000 per year:

16 percent of $6,000 ($960) *plus* 8 percent of $3,999 ($319.92) *plus* 4 percent of $39,999 ($1,599.96) for a total of $2,879.88. Divide that amount by 12 to determine the monthly child support amount of $239.99. Texas also allows for additional payments for healthcare and other adjustments.

Gross Income	1 Child	2 Children	3 Children	4 Children
First $6,000	16%	22%	26%	28%
$6,001-$10,000	8%	11%	13%	14%
$10,001+	4%	6%	6%	7%

NOTE: For 5 or more children, add an additional 2% for the first $6,000 in income; add an additional 1% for any amount from $6,001 to $10,000; and add an additional amount of 0.5% for income over $10,000.

Figure 4: Texas Child Support Percentage Table

The Melson Formula

At the time of printing, only three states used the Melson Formula[xxxvii] to determine child support: Delaware, Montana and Hawaii. Developed by The Honorable Elwood F. Melson, Jr., this model is considered fairer, as it takes into consideration both the parents' needs and the children's needs.

The formula enables parents to deduct a portion of their income to cover their own essential living expenses, ensuring they have sufficient funds to meet their basic needs. The next part of the formula designates a set amount for the child's basic needs based on the combined incomes of both parents.

Finally, the parties divide the cost of the child's primary support in proportion to their income, which is similar to the income shares model.

The Melson Formula also applies a Standard of Living Adjustment, as well as adjustments for special expenses, such as childcare, uncovered medical expenses and health insurance.

- Delaware's Child Support Guidelines Worksheet[xxxviii] (see endnote)
- Hawaii's Child Support Guidelines Worksheet[xxxix] (see endnote)
- Montana's Child Support Guidelines Worksheet[xl] (see endnote)

CHAPTER 18: SPOUSAL SUPPORT (ALIMONY)

Alimony, now commonly referred to as spousal support, helps a spouse in a lesser financial position recover after a divorce. Decades ago, when women were more likely to stay home to care for their families, alimony was a necessity. Now, in most cases, both spouses work, and sometimes the wife brings in more than the husband. It is common for men to receive alimony in a divorce; thus, the term is now spousal support. It allows the lower-earning spouse to maintain a reasonable standard of living until he or she can obtain the work experience or education required to improve his or her financial position.

Types of Spousal Support

Most states offer several types of support, including temporary and permanent spousal support. Over the years, permanent support has become less popular, especially since those who divorced often remarry. Various states may use different terms or offer additional types of spousal support; however, the following are the most common.

Types of spousal support include:

Temporary Spousal Support

Sometimes referred to as spousal support *pendente lite* or alimony *pendente lite,* courts typically order temporary support during the pendency of divorce proceedings to help the recipient cover living expenses until the case resolves.

Long-Term or Permanent Spousal Support

The court orders long-term spousal support as part of the final judgment of dissolution of marriage. Long-term spousal support, sometimes referred to as permanent spousal support, although it is rarely permanent, can last for a set period or indefinitely, depending on the parties' circumstances. Some states may not order indefinite or permanent support, and more are getting away from this type of alimony.

Courts typically reserve long-term support for long-term marriages when one spouse is unable to become self-sufficient due to age, health, or other factors.

Rehabilitative Spousal Support

Courts order rehabilitative support for a set period of time to help the recipient become self-sufficient, usually to give him or her time to obtain the education or job experience required to better him or herself.

Reimbursement Spousal Support

Courts may sometimes order one spouse to reimburse the other for education or career advancement when the receiving spouse puts his or her own education and/or career on hold for the sake of the marriage and to help the paying spouse improve his or her position.

Lump-Sum Spousal Support

A less common type of support, lump-sum spousal support, is a one-time payment instead of ongoing support. Courts may order a lump sum in certain circumstances, or the parties may request it or settle on it to provide a clean financial break. It is not common, as most people cannot come up with a lump sum of alimony at one time.

Eligibility and Application

The courts do not automatically order a spouse to pay alimony. Either spouse can request it, and the court may grant it based on statutory guidelines and the facts of the case.

Most states do not have a formula for the amount of spousal support awarded. It is generally at the court's discretion. However, the courts must review statutory factors against the facts of the case to determine whether to order support and, if so, how much.

Common factors the court reviews include:

- The requesting party has an actual need for support
- The paying party has the ability to pay support
- The duration of the marriage
- The standard of living established during the marriage
- The needs of each party after the entry of the final judgment
- The age of the parties
- The physical, mental and emotional condition of each party
- The resources available to each party
- The income of each party, including income generated from marital and nonmarital assets
- The earning capacity and educational levels of both parties
- Vocational skills of both parties
- Employability of both parties
- The contribution of each party to the marriage, including homemaking, education, childcare and career-building of the other party
- The responsibilities each party will have concerning minor children, with special consideration for a spouse caring for a child with a mental or physical disability
- Any other factor necessary for equity and justice between the parties

Duration and Modification

The court may order spousal support for a fixed term, or it could remain in effect until a specific event, such as the remarriage of the receiving party or the death of either party. Most states permit the modification or termination of spousal support if one of the parties experiences a significant change in circumstances unless the court orders non-modifiable support.

Tax Implications of Spousal Support

In the past, spousal support was considered taxable income to the recipient, which meant the paying party could claim it as a deduction. However, the Tax Cuts and Jobs Act, which Congress signed into law on December 22, 2017, made alimony nontaxable for recipients and nondeductible for payers at the federal level, starting with divorce and separation agreements finalized after December 31, 2018.

CHAPTER 19: HOME STUDIES AND PSYCHOLOGICAL EVALUATIONS

Critical tools in the family law arena include home studies and psychological evaluations. Attorneys and courts commonly use them in cases involving child custody, adoption and when someone alleges abuse and/or neglect against one or both parents.

The primary goal of both of these reports is to provide the court with objective, comprehensive assessments of the family environments and the psychological well-being of the parties involved.

Home Studies

A home study is a structured assessment by a licensed professional to evaluate the safety, stability and suitability of a home for a child. All states require them for adoptions, but courts will also order a home study in some custody cases. Requirements for foster homes may vary from state to state.

Components of a Home Study

A comprehensive home study[xli] is essential in certain custody cases. Home studies may include the following components, as supported by statutory requirements, government guidelines and leading adoption agencies:

- **Criminal Records**: All adult household members must undergo criminal background checks to identify any history of arrests or convictions that could pose a risk to the child's safety.

- **Child Abuse Registry**: Professionals conducting home studies also check state and national child abuse and neglect registries to ensure no member of the household has a substantial record of abuse or neglect.

- **References**: Those required to undergo a home study in a custody case must provide personal and professional references. The investigator uses these to assess character, parenting ability and suitability.

- **Interviews**: The investigator will conduct interviews with the parents, other adult members of the household and the children in the home. These interviews are in-depth and assess motivation, parenting philosophy and relationship dynamics. The children's interviews, when age-appropriate, help assess family dynamics.

- **Home Inspection**: During the home study, the investigator inspects the home for safety hazards, such as unsecured firearms, dangerous chemicals and/or unsafe structures. He or she also checks fire extinguishers, smoke detectors and emergency exits.

  Part of the inspection also includes the cleanliness and hygiene of the home, adequate living space, including sufficient privacy, and overall warmth, stability and the ability for the parent to meet the child's needs.

- **Income and Employment**: Parents will need to provide pay stubs and tax returns to confirm financial stability, verify their employment and show that they have the ability to provide for the child's essential needs and activities.

- **Medical and Psychological Health**: All household members may have to provide medical records to screen for communicable diseases or health issues that may affect caregiving. They may also have to submit evaluations or statements from mental health professionals to ensure emotional stability and the capacity to provide a supportive environment.

- **Family History and Parenting Experience**: A home study explores previous parenting experiences, the quality and stability of relationships with others in the household, including the children, and your reasons for seeking the type of custody you requested of the court.

In most states, the home study must be current, often within six months, and the parties must update it if circumstances change. Additionally, if the parties have one or more special needs children, the court may require additional assessment of a parent's capacity to care for the child.

Psychological Evaluations

A qualified mental health professional provides a comprehensive assessment of the parties' psychological well-being in certain custody disputes, including those with allegations of abuse and/or neglect, or if a parent or the court has concerns with parental fitness.

A court may order a psychological evaluation when one or both parents' mental health is in question or if one parent alleges the other parent is or was abusing or neglecting the child. In some cases, if a child's best interests require expert input, the court may also order a psychological evaluation. Judges, attorneys or guardians *ad litem* can request psych evals.

The Evaluation Process

The evaluator must be a licensed psychologist or psychiatrist. Some states may allow a qualified clinical social worker to conduct a psych eval. The mental health professional conducts clinical interviews with parents, children and sometimes teachers and caregivers. They use standardized tests to assess personality, mental health, parenting capacity and risk factors (Appendix III).

The evaluator observes how the parent and child interact with each other to assess the quality of their relationship and parenting skills, and reviews medical, educational and legal records. He or she may also interview third parties in relation to various records.

Psychological evaluations focus on the best interests of the child in addition to parental fitness. They are not designed to determine guilt or innocence, but to inform the court of the psychological, emotional and mental health factors affecting the case.

Once the evaluator completes the psychological evaluation, he or she compiles the findings and recommendations into a detailed report for the court. The court may use evaluations as evidence in hearings and trials, and often calls the evaluators to testify to their findings. The report can significantly influence the court's decision on legal and physical custody and visitation.

If the court orders a psychological evaluation, the parties should be honest, open and should cooperate throughout the process. Your attorney can help you better understand the process and can respond to findings.

If a party does not agree with the findings, he or she can contest the findings and request independent evaluations.

CHAPTER 20: RESTRAINING ORDERS IN FAMILY LAW

Protective orders, sometimes referred to as injunctions or restraining orders, are vital legal tools in family law designed to protect individuals from abuse and other harmful conduct. Restraining orders can be temporary or permanent. The court tailors them to address the specific risks and needs of the parties involved.

Types of Restraining Orders in Family Law

Most states recognize several types of restraining and protective orders, including:

- **Temporary Restraining Order (TRO)**: The court issues TROs quickly, typically without a hearing, to provide immediate protection or preserve the status quo until the courts can hold a formal hearing. They are common at the onset of divorce or custody proceedings and can prohibit actions such as selling marital assets, relocating children or altering insurance policies.

- **Order of Protection**: Specifically designed for cases involving domestic violence, threats or stalking. An order of protection can prohibit all contact, require an alleged abuser to move out of the marital home and grant temporary custody of the children to the petitioner in the domestic violence case. A violation can result in criminal charges.

- **No Contact Order**: The court typically issues no-contact orders in criminal cases, prohibiting the defendant from communicating with or approaching the alleged victim while the case is pending.
- **Civil Injunction for Harassment or Stalking**: Courts may issue civil injunctions for harassment or stalking in cases of repeated unwanted behavior that causes fear or distress, even if the parties are not in a qualifying domestic relationship.

Standard Provisions in Family Law Restraining Orders

A restraining order includes a variety of specific instructions that may vary from state to state. Some of the common provisions include:

- No contact by phone, email, mail, social media and/or in person
- Requires one party to stay a certain distance from the other party's home, place of employment, church and/or the child's school
- Prevents the sale, transfer and/or destruction of marital property
- Awards temporary custody and/or time-sharing arrangements
- Requires continued payment of marital bills or insurance premiums
- Orders the relinquishment of firearms
- Mandates attendance at counseling and/or treatment programs

Legal Basis and Process

The petitioner must demonstrate a credible threat of harm or a pattern of abusive, threatening or harassing behavior. Courts usually require evidence, such as documentation of abuse, threats or harassment and/or medical records where applicable. The process and standards of proof vary from state to state, but provide swift protection when necessary.

The Impact of Restraining Orders on Family Law Matters

A restraining order can significantly affect family law proceedings, including:

- **Child Custody**: The court may limit visitation or order supervised visitation if the restraining order involves the children.
- **Property and Finances**: Orders can freeze assets, mainly to prevent financial misconduct during the divorce proceedings.
- **Emotional and Legal Consequences**: The process is often emotionally taxing for both parties, but the primary goal is to ensure safety and prevent further harm.

Enforcement and Violations of Restraining Orders

The courts take violations of restraining orders seriously and may issue a warrant for an individual's arrest on criminal charges or hold the individual in contempt of court. A restraining order is enforceable across jurisdictions, providing broad protection to those in need.

CHAPTER 21: HANDLING COMPLEX ASSETS

Dividing complex assets, such as multiple real estate holdings, business interests and retirement accounts, is one of the most challenging aspects of family law, particularly in high-net-worth divorces. These cases often involve a wide range of valuable property and require careful planning, account valuation and strategic negotiation to ensure the parties receive a fair and equitable outcome.

Defining Complex Assets

Courts consider assets that go beyond typical marital property, such as the family home or joint checking accounts, as complex assets. Common examples include:

- Multiple real estate holdings, such as a primary residence, vacation home, rental properties and land
- Business interests, such as ownership in private companies and professional practices
- Investment portfolios, such as stocks, bonds, mutual funds and private equity
- Retirement accounts and pensions, including 401(k)s, IRAs and executive compensation packages
- Intellectual property, including copyrights, patents and trademarks

- Valuable personal property, such as collectibles, jewelry, art and luxury vehicles
- Trust funds
- Inheritances

Complex property follows the same rules to determine whether it is marital property or separate property. Some assets, such as retirement accounts or rental properties, may have both marital and individual components. These assets may have started as separate property; however, if the parties used marital funds for the upkeep of the property or, in the case of financial accounts, used marital funds to increase the value of the asset, a portion of these assets often becomes marital and requires special division.

Valuation of Complex Assets

The accurate valuation of these assets is essential for equitable distribution, often requiring the services of professional appraisers, forensic accountants, actuaries, or other specialists. Valuations need to reflect the market value as of the date of separation or another legally relevant date and may need to account for future appreciation, tax consequences, and liquidity.

Division Strategies

The parties can divide complex assets in several ways. However, if they cannot agree on property division, the court will step in and make those decisions. Couples have several options available for asset division, including:

- **In-Kind Division**: Splitting the assets is more common with property that is easier to liquidate, such as specific stocks, retirement accounts or individually owned bank accounts.

- **Buyout**: One spouse retains the asset and compensates the other for his or her share. This type of division is common for real estate, business interests and collections.

- **Sell and Split**: The parties can opt to sell the asset and divide the proceeds. This type of division is beneficial to real estate or collections.

- **Offsetting Assets**: Each spouse takes different assets of equivalent value to balance the division of assets. For example, one spouse keeps the business, and the other keeps more investment accounts or a vacation property.

The parties typically need to find creative solutions, mainly when assets cannot be liquidated or have sentimental value.

Special Considerations for Specific Assets

Some assets may require special consideration for valuation, including:

- **Real Estate**: Those who own real estate, especially high-value properties, multiple properties, or investment properties, may require various appraisals, consideration of rental income, and analysis of tax implications on sale.

- **Businesses**: Division depends on the level of involvement by each spouse, whether you can split the business or must sell it, and future earning potential.

- **Investments**: Parties must consider fluctuating values and tax consequences, especially for restricted stocks or deferred compensation.

- **Retirement Accounts**: Most retirement accounts require a Qualified Domestic Relations Order (QDRO) to avoid penalties and ensure proper transfer of funds.

- **Intellectual Property**: Valuation can be complex due to the potential for future income and marketability.

- **Trusts and Inheritances**: While trusts and inheritances are typically considered separate property in most states, commingling can convert them into marital property. For example, depositing cash from an inheritance into a joint account makes it marital property.

Tax Implications

In most cases, assets transferred in a divorce are non-taxable. However, if the only way to equitably divide an asset is to sell it or liquidate investments, it can trigger significant taxes and penalties. Strategic planning can minimize tax liabilities and preserve wealth for both parties.

The Role of Professionals

When planning a divorce, it is essential to work with experienced family law attorneys. If you have complex assets, ensure the attorney has experience with complex asset division. Financial advisors, planners, and forensic accountants can also utilize their expertise to minimize taxes and penalties by creating a strategic plan.

Finally, when choosing appraisers and valuation experts, ensure they have years of experience, as a mistake could result in a significant financial loss for you and your spouse. When these professionals work together, they help ensure that you identify all of your property, value it, and divide it in accordance with the law and the parties' best interests.

Negotiation and Settlement for Divorces with High Assets

Whenever possible, reach an agreement outside of court, as it offers more flexibility and privacy. However, if negotiations fail, the court divides the assets based on factors such as each spouse's contributions, future needs, and the overall fairness of the proposed division.

CHAPTER 22: THE IMPACT OF DIVORCE ON WILLS, INSURANCE AND BENEFICIARY DESIGNATIONS

Divorce is a major life event that alters personal relationships and finances. It also has significant legal consequences for estate planning, insurance and beneficiary designations. Overlooking these issues can lead to unintended outcomes, such as an ex-spouse inheriting assets or retaining control over important decisions.

One of the first steps individuals should take when planning for divorce is to consult with an estate planning attorney to update their estate plans.

Divorce and Wills

In most states, divorce automatically revokes any gifts or appointments made to a former spouse in a will unless the will explicitly states otherwise. If the will names an alternate beneficiary, that person inherits the item. If not, the state's intestacy laws apply as if the grantor had not made a will.

Some states have laws that also revoke gifts to relatives of former spouses. Revocation of gifts to former spouses does not invalidate the rest of the will.

Divorce may also revoke the appointment of a named executor. If the will does not name an alternate, the court will appoint one.

If a spouse dies during the divorce process or separation, the law typically does not revoke gifts; therefore, it is essential that individuals update their estate plans as soon as possible, preferably before separation or the filing of the petition for dissolution.

Do not forget to update powers of attorney, living wills and other estate planning documents.

State	Statute	State	Statute	State	Statute
AL	Ala. Code §43-8-137	AK	Alaska Stat. §13.12.804	AZ	Ariz. Rev. Stat. §14-2804
AR	Ark. Code Ann. §28-25-109	CA	Cal. Probate Code §6122	CO	Colo. Rev. Stat. § 15-11-804
CT	Conn. Gen. Stat. § 45a-257c	DE	Del. Code Ann. tit. 12, § 209	FL	Fla. Stat. § 732.507(2)
GA	Ga. Code Ann. § 53-4-49	HI	Haw. Rev. Stat. § 560:2-804	ID	Idaho Code § 15-2-804
IL	755 Ill. Comp. Stat. 5/4-7(b)	IN	Ind. Code § 29-1-5-8	IA	Iowa Code § 633.271
KS	Kan. Stat. Ann. § 59-610	KY	Ky. Rev. Stat. Ann. § 394.092	LA	La. Civ. Code Ann. art. 1608
ME	18-C Me. Rev. Stat. Ann. § 2-804	MD	Md. Code Ann., Est. & Trusts § 4-105(4)	MA	Mass. Gen. Laws ch. 191, § 9
MI	Mich. Comp. Laws § 700.2807	MN	Minn. Stat. § 524.2-804	MS	Miss. Code Ann. § 91-5-3
MO	Mo. Rev. Stat. § 474.420	MT	Mont. Code Ann. § 72-2-814	NE	Neb. Rev. Stat. § 30-2333
NV	Nev. Rev. Stat. § 133.115	NH	N.H. Rev. Stat. Ann. § 551:13	NJ	N.J. Stat. Ann. § 3B:3-14
NM	N.M. Stat. Ann. § 45-2-804	NY	N.Y. Est. Powers & Trusts Law § 5-1.4	NC	N.C. Gen. Stat. § 31-5.4
ND	N.D. Cent. Code § 30.1-10-04	OH	Ohio Rev. Code Ann. § 2107.33	OK	Okla. Stat. tit. 84, § 114
OR	Or. Rev. Stat. § 112.315	PA	20 Pa. Cons. Stat. § 2507(2)	RI	R.I. Gen. Laws § 33-5-9
SC	S.C. Code Ann. § 62-2-507	SD	S.D. Codified Laws § 29A-2-804	TN	Tenn. Code Ann. § 32-1-202
TX	Tex. Est. Code § 123.001	UT	Utah Code Ann. § 75-2-804	VT	Vt. Stat. Ann. tit. 14, § 320
VA	Va. Code Ann. § 64.2-412	WA	Wash. Rev. Code § 11.12.051	WV	W. Va. Code § 41-1-6
WI	Wis. Stat. § 854.15	WY	Wyo. Stat. Ann. § 2-6-112		

Figure 5: State Codes for Revocation Statute

Divorce and Insurance Policies

Courts may require at least one of the parties—usually the spouse paying support—to maintain or purchase life insurance as part of a divorce settlement. The policy serves as financial protection for the ex-spouse or minor children. It is more common for the court to order one or both parties to purchase life insurance if one spouse is paying child and spousal support; however, courts can also order it even when the parties do not have children or are not paying spousal support.

If an individual has insurance policies that the court did not order, the policyholder must change the beneficiary, as divorce does not automatically revoke the beneficiary as it does with an estate plan. If you do not update the beneficiary prior to filing for divorce, you should update it as soon as the divorce finalizes.

If the court orders you to name a specific beneficiary on the insurance policy, you must name that person.

Joint and Single Insurance Policies

If you have a joint insurance policy, you can handle it by:

- Having one party take over the policy,
- Separating the policy, if the insurance company allows it, or
- Cancelling the policy and obtaining a new individual policy for each party.

Always research before making a decision, as costs and terms may change when you purchase a new policy, especially terms related to age or your health.

Beneficiary Designations and Wills

Beneficiary designations on investment accounts, retirement accounts, bank accounts, and life insurance override instructions in a will or trust. If you forget to change the beneficiary and you die, your ex-spouse will receive the proceeds of the account.

In most cases, it is the individual's responsibility to update the beneficiary designation after divorce. Contact insurance companies, retirement plan administrators and financial institutions to request a new beneficiary designation form. Always follow up to ensure the institution processed your request.

CHAPTER 23: ATTORNEY FEES AND SELF-REPRESENTATION

Family law cases often involve significant legal and financial decisions. One major concern for many individuals is the cost of legal representation. Understanding how attorney fees work, including what influences the amount, and the alternatives to hiring an attorney, such as self-representation, is essential for anyone facing a family law issue.

Attorney fees can vary widely based on several factors, including:

- **Type and Complexity of the Case**: Divorce, support, and custody cases have unique legal requirements and complexities, including property distribution and the cooperation of the parties, which can affect the amount of work required and, consequently, the cost.

- **Attorney Experience and Reputation**: More experienced attorneys and those with specialized experience, such as handling high-value cases or cases involving domestic violence, generally command higher fees.

- **Geographic Location**: Attorney fees differ significantly by state and even by city.

- **Billing Structure**: Attorneys may charge by the hour, require a retainer or offer flat fees for certain services.

Always discuss the attorney's fees during your initial consultation.

Allocation of Attorney Fees in a Divorce Case

Generally, each spouse pays his or her own attorney fees. However, in some circumstances, such as when a spouse stays home to care for the children and manage the household, he or she may not have an income or other resources to pay an attorney.

In these cases, the non-working spouse may request that the other spouse pay attorney fees as part of the relief requested in the petition. In this case, the court may order the other party to pay the non-working spouse's attorney fees. The court may also order one spouse to pay the other spouse's attorney fees in cases where one party was engaged in marital misconduct, especially if it unnecessarily increases legal costs.

Additionally, in some child custody cases, the court may order the losing party to reimburse the other party's attorney fees.

Sometimes, one party may agree to pay the other's attorney fees as part of a settlement.

Managing and Reducing Attorney Fees

You can manage and potentially reduce attorney fees by taking the following steps:

- **Effective Communication**: Creating an outline of your questions can help you create clear, organized communication, which can reduce your billable hours.
- **Alternative Dispute Resolution**: Mediation or collaborative law is sometimes less expensive than litigation.
- **Legal Tasks**: Handling some paperwork yourself can lower costs. For example, when preparing discovery, organizing it and making the requisite number of copies can save you quite a bit.
- **Payment Plan and Financial Assistance**: Some attorneys offer payment plans or sliding-scale fees for clients with limited means.

Self-Representation (*Pro Se* Representation)

Appearing in court without an attorney is an option in all family law matters. While there are benefits to it, such as cost savings and managing your own case, we do not recommend it, as the disadvantages outweigh the advantages.

Most laypeople lack sufficient knowledge of the law to represent themselves effectively. The court cannot give you legal advice. One mistake can end up costing you significantly more than you might have paid an attorney.

Furthermore, family law has several filing deadlines. If you miss one, it could jeopardize your case. The risk of unfavorable outcomes is high if you do not have legal expertise.

Going through a divorce—even one you wanted—is stressful enough without adding the stress of managing your own case.

However, *pro se* representation may be appropriate if your case does not have significant assets, debts or custody disputes.

If you have children and property, and you and your spouse can agree on everything, it is better to have an attorney represent you, as a poorly drafted settlement agreement can also cost you significantly.

CHAPTER 24: MODIFICATION OF CUSTODY AND SUPPORT ORDERS

In some cases, you may have to request a modification of a custody order, child support order or a spousal support order. Over time, circumstances can change, whether they are financial or not.

Child custody orders provide stability and serve the best interests of the child; however, circumstances often change, which necessitate adjustments to custody orders. A parent's job may require a transfer, a parent may suffer a serious illness, or may even become involved in a situation where it is no longer safe for the child to stay with that parent.

Courts recognize the need for changes and allow custody modifications when one of the parties exhibits a substantial change in circumstances that significantly affects the child's welfare.

Either party can file a motion or petition to modify a custody order, regardless of which parent the change affects. For example, if the custodial parent allows a significant other to move in, and he or she is abusive, the other parent can ask the court to modify the custody order.

Legal Standard for Modification

Regardless of the issue, whether it is spousal support, child support or child custody, the legal standard for modification remains the same. The parent seeking the modification must demonstrate a material change in circumstances since the court issued the original order.

A court will not grant modifications for minor or temporary changes—the change must be ongoing and substantial[xlii].

Common Reasons for Modification

When you believe a change is ongoing and material, you can request a modification from the court. However, you will need to prove the change and that it affects the child's well-being. An attorney can ensure you understand your rights and the law on modification matters.

Some of the common reasons for requesting a modification of custody or support orders include:

- **Relocation**: When a parent must move due to work, family support or other reasons, and the move affects the child's living arrangements or ability to maintain a relationship with both parents.

- **Parental Fitness or Lifestyle**: Significant changes such as a parent's employment, health or living situation and issues related to criminal activity or substance abuse.

- **Child's Needs or Preferences**: The child's educational, medical or emotional needs change, or the child expresses a preference for a different arrangement.

- **Evidence of Abuse or Neglect**: New information about abuse, neglect or domestic violence can prompt immediate modification to protect the child. If you suspect abuse or neglect, contact an experienced attorney as soon as possible. Depending on the severity of the situation, your attorney may be able to file an emergency order on your behalf.

- **Financial Reasons**: When a parent experiences a substantial change in their financial situation, such as an increase in income, job loss, or an inability to provide for the child's needs, you can request a modification, especially if it affects a child's stability or access to essential care.

- **Parental Abduction or Noncompliance**: If a parent absconds with the child to another state or country without the court's approval or repeatedly violates the custody order, you can ask the court to intervene by requesting a modification of the custody order to protect the child's best interests. Abduction is an emergency, especially if you do not know where your ex-spouse took your child.

The Modification Process and Jurisdictional Issues

The modification process starts with one parent filing a petition for modification, usually in the same court that issued the final judgment. Both parents have the opportunity to present evidence, including documentation, testimony and professional evaluations to support their position.

If the parents can agree on the changes, they can submit a new parenting plan for the court's approval. If not, the court holds a hearing and decides based on the evidence and the child's best interests.

If a parent takes a child to another jurisdiction without approval from the other parent or the court, the original court can enforce its order and sanction the offending parent.

Once the court approves a modification, the new order is legally binding. Parents must comply with its terms. If not, the court can issue sanctions, remove custody or time-sharing from the offending parent, or require supervised visitation to enforce compliance.

CHAPTER 25: PRACTICAL TIPS FOR PARENTS

Divorce is an emotional time for all involved. Even when parents avoid arguing in front of children, many sense tension in the household. Some practical tips for parents to make the divorce and custody process as smooth as possible include:

- Prioritize the child's best interests above your own preferences or grievances. Focus on what will support your child's well-being and stability.

- Avoid speaking negatively about the other parent in front of your child, on social media, or in any communication that the other parent could use in court. Courts look for parents who encourage a positive relationship between the child and the other parent.

- Never withhold visitation or communication with the other parent unless you have genuine safety concerns.

- Always follow court orders and support the child's relationship with the other parent.

- Maintain open, constructive and respectful communication with the other parent, even when disagreements arise. Demonstrating a willingness to cooperate can influence custody decisions.

- Keep detailed records of parenting time, communications and incidents related to the child's care and interactions with the other parent. This documentation can be vital in court.
- Non-compliance with custody and other court orders can damage your credibility and impact future custody decisions.
- Always present yourself as stable and reliable. Maintain steady employment and provide a safe home for your child.
- Ensure your child attends school every day he or she is not genuinely sick.
- Ensure your child attends all scheduled medical appointments.
- Always avoid involving your child in adult conflicts or using him or her as a messenger between you and the other parent.
- Shield your child from litigation and emotional disputes.
- Seek support from mental health professionals, counselors or support groups to help manage stress and emotions during and after the custody process.
- Always be flexible and willing to adjust your parenting schedule to accommodate your child's activities and changing needs. Remember, your child's needs come first.
- Never make false allegations or exaggerate claims about the other parent.
- Continue to encourage and support your child's relationship with the other parent after the divorce.
- Revisit the parenting plan as your child grows and circumstances change.
- Cooperate and communicate respectfully with the other parent.
- Focus on the child's needs, not parental conflict.
- Seek legal advice if you are considering modifying the custody order, child support or if you are relocating.

CHAPTER 26: THE DIVORCE PROCESS: STEP-BY-STEP

Filing for divorce can seem overwhelming once you see the amount of paperwork that you need to do. Even with the help of an attorney, it can be overwhelming, especially once you reach the discovery process.

All states offer uncontested divorce, which is what you file if you and your spouse agree on all aspects of the divorce. Regardless of the process you choose, the initial steps are the same. Taking certain steps prior to filing for divorce can help smooth the process and reduce some of the stress associated with it.

Steps to Take Prior to the Divorce

If you file, your attorney will provide you with an intake sheet that requests a significant amount of information. Review the intake sheet, filling in all the information you have. On a second read-through, gather the documents requested. Keep them in the order requested.

For this set of documents, you will need one copy for the attorney. Never send in originals unless specifically requested. You can save money by making the copies yourself. In most cases, the attorney will return the original, so make a copy of it and send both the copy and the original.

You can also start gathering financial information at this stage. Depending on your attorney's process, he or she may or may not request discovery at this point. Some attorneys wait until the discovery process starts. See Part II of this book to learn how to gather and organize discovery.

Uncontested Divorce Step-by-Step

If you and your spouse agree on all aspects of the divorce, you can file an uncontested divorce. While you can download the forms from your court's website and file them yourself, you will not receive a robust settlement agreement. We recommend retaining an attorney who can draft an extensive settlement agreement that better protects your rights.

Even if the divorce is amicable, you don't know what will happen in the future, especially when you co-parent.

Throughout all the steps, your attorney will complete the necessary documents for you. However, if you decide to file *pro se*, you will have to complete the documents.

STEP 1: Complete the Civil Cover Sheet and other documents the court may request in the uncontested divorce process. If you retain an attorney, the attorney will do this for you. The Civil Cover Sheet tells the clerk what kind of case you are filing. It also tells the clerk whether you are filing in the appropriate jurisdiction.

STEP 2: Complete the Petition for Dissolution of Marriage. Depending on your state, this document could have a different name, such as 'Petition for Divorce' or 'Complaint.' The information required for the petition varies by state, but is generally similar in most. You will need:

- Your and your spouse's full legal names.
- Your spouse's maiden name.
- Birthdates for you, your spouse and your children.
- Home and mailing addresses for you and your spouse.
- Date of marriage.
- Location (city, county and state) of marriage.
- Date of separation.

- Location (city, county and state) of separation.
- Residency information—proof that at least one spouse meets the state's residency requirements, including how long you or your spouse lived in the state or county.
- Grounds for divorce—in most states, this will be irreconcilable differences for an uncontested divorce (no fault).
- Each child's full legal name, birthdate and current address.
- Requests for relief are what you are asking for in the divorce. In an uncontested divorce, these items should match what you have agreed upon in the Marital Settlement Agreement. They include custody, visitation, property division, child support, spousal support and restoration of a former name.
- Disclosure of assets, debts, income and expenses. Some states may include this information in the petition, but most require a separate financial affidavit.
- Details about current health insurance coverage for both parties and the children.
- Statement regarding responsibility for joint debts.
- Proof of completion of the parenting class if you have minor children. In most states, you file this as a separate document; however, some may request it in the petition.
- Certificate of verification and non-collusion—a sworn statement that the information is true and correct and the filing is not for improper purposes.
- Signature and notarization.

STEP 3: Complete the respondent's answer. Some attorneys include this document in the petition for uncontested divorces, but most states' forms include a separate answer.

STEP 4: Complete the Notice of Social Security Numbers. You will need your own, your spouse's, and your children's social security numbers.

STEP 5: Complete the Uniform Child-Custody Jurisdiction and Enforcement Act (UCCJEA) form. This is often contained in the Petition for Dissolution of Marriage, but may be a separate document. You will need your children's full legal names, dates of birth, current address and addresses for the past five years.

STEP 6: Complete the Family Law Financial Affidavit. You will need a list of all assets, liabilities and expenses. Use fair market values and appraised values unless instructed otherwise. For step-by-step instructions, see Part II: Discovery.

STEP 7: Complete the Waiver of Discovery. If your state does not allow you to waive discovery in an uncontested divorce, complete the mandatory disclosure forms.

STEP 8: Complete the Marital Settlement Agreement. We strongly advise that you retain an attorney to draft a settlement agreement, as it will have better protections for your rights than the form provides.

STEP 9: Complete any information required on the proposed final judgment.

STEP 10: Sign and date all documents. If a document requires a notarized signature, do not sign it until you are in front of a notary.

STEP 11: Make two copies of each document. Give one copy to the respondent and keep one copy.

STEP 12: Look up the filing fee for your state. Each state, and often, each county, has its own filing fee. You can look up this information on the court's website or call the clerk for this information. Check the court's website or ask the clerk about the forms of payment the court accepts.

STEP 13: File the documents with the clerk. You may have to file them in person. However, some states may have electronic access for the general public. You will find this information on the clerk's website.

STEP 14: Attend the uncontested final hearing. In some states, only one person needs to attend to "prove up" the divorce. The amount of time before the court schedules the final hearing depends on several factors, including your state's waiting period and the case log at the court. You can always check with the clerk if you have not received a Notice of Hearing after the waiting period, plus a few weeks have expired.

STEP 15: Attend the final hearing. Once the judge executes and files the final judgment, your divorce is final, except in states where the law requires a waiting period after the court signs the decree/final judgment. You should receive a copy of the final judgment, which will incorporate the marital settlement agreement.

Contested Divorce Step-by-Step

A contested divorce is when the parties cannot agree on one or more aspects of the divorce, including property division, child custody, spousal support and child support. While every state has statutes that dictate how much child support each parent contributes, parties often disagree about the amount of resources the other party has, especially if one or both parties' income is from a business.

In some cases, the parties agree on all but one factor—and that one thing makes the divorce contested. You can sign a marital settlement agreement for everything you agree on, but unless you can negotiate the portion you do not agree on, the courts consider the divorce contested.

The divorce process has several deadlines, including the time to file an answer to the petition, court-ordered deadlines for filing certain pleadings or responses to those pleadings, discovery deadlines, and pretrial and trial deadlines.

Meeting these deadlines can often add to an already stressful process. You can make the process smoother and less stressful if you take specific steps prior to filing the divorce petition.

> **We do not recommend filing a contested divorce *pro se*, especially for high-asset divorces or those involving custody battles, as mistakes can be costly and potentially lead to unfavorable outcomes.**

STEP 1: Review the discovery process in Part II of *Family Law Basics*. Gather all documents required for the discovery process.

STEP 2: Organize the documents as suggested in Part II of *Family Law Basics*.

STEP 3: To save money, make copies of the documents as directed in Part II of *Family Law Basics*.

STEP 4: Gather all necessary information to complete the initial documents required to file the petition. You will need:

- Your and your spouse's full legal names.

- Your spouse's maiden name.

- Birthdates for you, your spouse and your children.

- Home and mailing addresses for you and your spouse.

- Date of marriage.

- Location (city, county and state) of marriage.

- Date of separation.

- Location (city, county and state) of separation.

- Residency information—proof that at least one spouse meets the state's residency requirements, including how long you or your spouse lived in the state or county.

- Grounds for divorce—in most states, this will be irreconcilable differences for an uncontested divorce (no fault).

- Each child's full legal name, birthdate and current address.

- Requests for relief are what you are asking for in the divorce. In an uncontested divorce, these items should match what you have agreed upon in the Marital Settlement Agreement. They include custody, visitation, property division, child support, spousal support and restoration of a former name.

- Disclosure of assets, debts, income and expenses. Some states may include this information in the petition, but most require a separate family law financial affidavit.

- Details about current health insurance coverage for both parties and the children.

- Statement regarding responsibility for joint debts.

- Proof of completion of the parenting class if you have minor children. In most states, you file this as a separate document; however, some may request it in the petition.

- Certificate of verification and non-collusion—a sworn statement that the information is true and correct and the filing is not for improper purposes.

- Signature and notarization.

STEP 5: Locate and retain an experienced family law attorney. You can ask for references from family and friends and check online reviews. Set an initial consultation with at least three attorneys and choose the lawyer who you feel has the best experience and case outcomes, and one who you feel comfortable with on a personal level. Do not skimp on the cost of the attorney. A poor lawyer is sometimes worse than not having one at all.

STEP 6: Complete the petition, civil cover sheet and summons. If you retain an attorney, he or she will do this for you. In this case, review the petition to ensure the attorney included everything you requested. ***You cannot go back and add something you think of later.***

STEP 7: Sign the documents and make three copies of the summons and petition. Make one copy of the civil cover sheet.

STEP 8: File the documents with the clerk, who will sign the summons. The court keeps the original, stamps a copy for you, a copy for the respondent, and, in some cases, a third copy for the process server.

STEP 9: Wait for the process server or sheriff to serve the respondent.

STEP 10: When the process server returns the notice of service, file it with the clerk along with a Notice of Filing Proof of Service. Be sure to make a copy of the Notice of Filing and the Proof of Service for yourself.

STEP 11: Wait for the respondent to file an Answer. The respondent must file an answer within the set number of days specified on the summons. He or she may file a counter-petition at the same time or may reserve the right to file a counter-petition at a later date.

STEP 12: File an answer to the counter-petition once you receive it.

STEP 13: File the Mandatory Disclosure request.

STEP 14: Forward your disclosure to the respondent and file the Notice of Filing Mandatory Disclosure.

STEP 15: If you need additional information or you know the respondent has not forwarded all required documents, you can file a Request for Production of Documents.

STEP 16: If necessary, file Interrogatories and Requests for Admissions.

STEP 17: Attend mediation. Some states and/or counties require the parties to attempt mediation. You can use a court-sponsored program or private mediation. While private mediation is more costly, you often have a better outcome with a private mediator.

STEP 18: If you were able to agree on all outstanding aspects of the divorce, the mediator or your attorney will draft a marital settlement agreement. Review the settlement agreement and sign it.

STEP 19: If mediation was not successful, prepare for litigation (trial).

During the entire process, you can file additional motions, including motions for temporary relief, motions to compel discovery and other motions as necessary.

Preparing for Trial

At this juncture, your case can go one of two ways. If you were able to agree on all aspects of the divorce, file the marital settlement agreement with a proposed final judgment of dissolution of marriage (or final decree, whichever terminology your state uses). Set an uncontested divorce hearing with the court.

Depending on your state's laws, one or both parties may attend the uncontested final hearing to prove up the divorce.

If you are unable to reach an agreement, schedule the pre-trial hearing with the court. At the pre-trial hearing, the court ensures both sides are ready for trial. It also determines how many hours you may need for a trial.

The court will instruct you to file additional documents, including a witness list. It may also hear any outstanding motions that are still relevant. Finally, the court will set a trial date.

> **If you have come this far without an attorney, we recommend that you retain an attorney for the trial. You will need an extensive understanding of your state's family laws to proceed and expect a favorable outcome, although retaining an attorney does not guarantee a favorable outcome, depending on your circumstances. It does increase the odds of reaching a favorable outcome.**

Once the court enters the final judgment, except in cases where states have a waiting period *after* the entry of the final judgment, your divorce is finalized.

CHAPTER 27: PRENUPTIAL AND POSTNUPTIAL AGREEMENTS

Prenuptial (prenups) and postnuptial (postnups) agreements are legally binding contracts that couples use to define their financial rights and responsibilities in marriage. They also use them as terms for property division and spousal support in the event of divorce or death.

The parties sign a **prenup** before the marriage to specify how the parties handle assets, debts and, in some instances, spousal support should the marriage end. These agreements protect each party's individual financial interests and clarify property division, inheritance rights and spousal support.

A **postnup** does the same thing, except the parties sign it after they enter into marriage to address changes in financial circumstances, clarify ownership of new assets and/or modify previous agreements.

Both parties must provide full financial disclosure and voluntarily consent to these agreements. Both types of agreements must also be in writing to be enforceable. Prenups and postnups cannot address child custody or child support.

Overview of the Role of Prenuptial and Postnuptial Agreements in Modern Family Law

Prenups and postnups have become increasingly common in modern family law, playing a significant role. The primary functions of these agreements include:

- **Asset Protection**: Protection of assets before or during the marriage. Assets may include real estate, business interests, investments and/or inheritances, especially when one party has significantly more assets than the future spouse.

- **Debt Allocation**: Specify how the parties will handle existing and future debts, ensuring that one spouse does not become unfairly burdened by the other's liabilities in the event of divorce or separation.

- **Estate Planning**: Clarify inheritance rights and the distribution of property upon death, especially in blended families or when one or both spouses have children from prior relationships. Prenups and postnups can also waive a spouse's right to claim an elective share of the other's estate, providing certainty for estate planning purposes.

- **Financial Transparency and Planning**: By requiring both parties to disclose their assets and liabilities, prenups and postnups promote honesty and open communication about finances, which can help prevent misunderstanding and future disputes.

- **Reducing Litigation and Uncertainty**: Clear, pre-arranged terms for property division and spousal support can minimize conflict and reduce the time and expense involved in divorce proceedings.

Prenuptial Agreement Legal Basis and Key Requirements

All 50 states recognize prenuptial agreements, which are effective upon marriage. State statutes govern these agreements, and many states have adopted the Uniform Premarital Agreement Act (UPAA), a multistate law enacted to enforce consistency in prenuptial agreements[xliii] [xliv].

The key requirements of a prenuptial agreement include:

- A prenup must be in writing and signed by both parties. Some states may require notarized signatures.

- Both parties must provide full and fair disclosure of assets, debts and income.

- Both parties must voluntarily enter into the agreement without duress, fraud or undue influence.

- Always seek independent legal counsel (each party has his or her own attorney to avoid a conflict of interest). Attorneys are not required but strongly advised.

- Must not contain provisions contrary to public policy, for example, child custody and support.

- Must follow state-specific formalities, such as notarization and/or witnesses.

Enforceability and Limitations of Prenuptial Agreements

The courts will review prenuptial agreements to ensure they are fair and enforceable. If the parties move to a new state, the courts also review choice-of-law jurisdictional clauses and their impact.

Each state has its own laws regarding prenuptial agreements, so the court also checks to ensure the agreement meets state-specific statutes.

Postnuptial Agreement Legal Basis and Key Requirements

Not all, but most states recognize postnuptial agreements—those entered into between spouses after they marry. Additionally, most states have varying requirements and enforceability standards. A postnuptial agreement has the same primary functions and key requirements as a prenuptial agreement.

Standard provisions (across states) in postnuptial agreements include:

- Division of property and debts acquired prior to and during the marriage.

- Business ownership acquired after the parties marry.

- Spousal support and financial arrangements in case of divorce or death.

- Provisions for significant life changes, such as having children, inheritances and business ventures.

Enforceability and Limitations of Postnuptial Agreements

The basic enforceability of postnuptial agreements is the same as it is for prenuptial agreements, with the added warning that timing and the circumstances of the execution of a postnuptial agreement can affect its enforceability.

It is crucial that both parties retain an experienced family law attorney for legal advice regarding postnuptial agreements. They should use separate attorneys to avoid a conflict of interest situation.

The parties should also consider creating an estate plan so that they can coordinate the postnuptial agreement with it. These agreements also need periodic review and updates, especially after major life events, just as an estate plan does.

PART 11:
FAMILY LAW BASICS: DISCOVERY

CHAPTER 28: INTRODUCTION TO FAMILY LAW DISCOVERY

Your attorney hands you a stack of discovery documents, including mandatory disclosure, interrogatories and requests for admissions. As you page through them, it may become overwhelming, seemingly impossible to complete the myriad of discovery requests in the allotted time.

You can make quick work of the discovery process by taking it one step at a time and remaining organized.

Types of Discovery Requests in Family Law Cases

The family law process uses discovery to obtain information and evidence from the parties to prepare for trial or settlement. Each type of discovery is essential, but not every case requires every type of discovery. In some cases, you'll only need to respond to the initial discovery request, titled "Mandatory Disclosure."

In other cases, especially cases with significant assets or those in a custody battle, you may need to complete interrogatories, requests for production of documents and/or requests for admissions.

In some states, a Request for Production of Documents and "mandatory disclosure" are one and the same. In other cases, attorneys may send mandatory disclosures. However, when the party fails to provide all the documents or the attorney suspects that the other party is withholding documents, the attorney may also send a specific request for the production of documents.

Why Discovery is Important

Discovery may seem overwhelming, but it is imperative that both parties provide all the required and applicable documents. It is the only way to ensure equitable distribution between the parties. It is the backbone of any family law case, serving as the formal process through which both parties gather and exchange essential information and evidence.

The discovery process does not punish or invade privacy—it ensures fairness and transparency for both parties. Issues such as property division, child support and custody hinge on accurate information that discovery provides.

By requiring both parties to provide all relevant documents, including financial records, property deeds, debts and evidence related to children, discovery uncovers the true scope of the marital estate and each party's circumstances.

The process prevents either side from hiding assets or withholding important details, which is vital for achieving an equitable distribution of property and a just resolution to other contested issues.

Discovery also helps identify key issues in disputes, streamlines settlement negotiations, and minimizes surprises at trial by ensuring both sides are aware of the strengths and weaknesses of their cases.

Courts take the discovery process seriously. Failing to comply can result in penalties, sanctions, or even losing the case by default.

CHAPTER 29: FAMILY LAW FINANCIAL AFFIDAVIT

While the Family Law Financial Affidavit is often one of the first documents filed after the respondent files his or her answer, it is part of the discovery process. Each state has its own financial affidavit, and we will use Florida's as an example.

Since this is an affidavit, you must sign it in front of a notary, and it must be true and correct to the best of your knowledge. Most financial affidavit uses *gross income*—the amount before your employer takes out taxes and other deductions.

To compute gross monthly income amounts:

- **Paid Hourly**: Hourly amount times the number of hours you work per week for the weekly amount. Multiply the weekly amount by 52 to get the yearly amount. Finally, divide the yearly amount by 12 for the average monthly amount.

- **Daily**: If your employer pays you daily, compute the monthly amount by multiplying the amount your employer pays you per day by the number of days you work each week for the weekly amount. Multiply that number by 52 to get your yearly pay. Divide that number by 12 for your average monthly pay.

- **Weekly**: Multiply your gross weekly pay by 52 and then divide it by 12 to obtain your average gross monthly income.
- **Bi-Weekly**: If you receive a paycheck every two weeks, multiply your bi-weekly gross income by 26 and then divide by 12 for the average monthly gross income.
- **Semi-Monthly**: If you receive a paycheck twice per month, usually on the same days (e.g., the 1st and the 15th), multiply the gross amount of your check by two for your monthly gross pay.

Section I: Income

The 'Income' section requires your full legal name, age and occupation. You must also check the appropriate box stating whether you are unemployed or employed. If you are employed, provide your employer's name, address and telephone number, your pay rate and how often you receive a paycheck.

If you have a second job, you must also provide the same information for that job.

The 'Income' section offers a third option for retirees. If you retired, provide the date you retired, the employer you retired from and the employer's address and telephone number.

Finally, provide your gross income and the year you earned it. If you know your spouse's gross income, you can also provide that information.

Present Monthly Gross Income

The second part of Section I asks for various types of income. Complete all applicable fields with a *__monthly__* amount. Go through this section carefully, as it includes several forms of income, including but not limited to bonuses, commissions, royalties, spousal support, reimbursed expenses, interest and dividends, retirement income, disability benefits, income from government programs and more.

Add the amounts on the lines and total them at the bottom for your total present monthly gross income.

Present Monthly Deductions

Use the same method you used to figure out your monthly gross income to compute monthly deductions. You should know your federal tax filing status and the number of dependents you claim. Be sure to enter **all** monthly deductions.

Subtract the total deductions from your gross income to obtain your present monthly net income.

Section II: Average Monthly Expenses

The amounts for your average monthly expenses can be estimated or proposed. If you are currently separated, you can estimate your expenses, as they vary from month to month. For example, your electric bill may be $150 during the summer, but it could be $500 during the winter.

Most utilities offer online access, allowing you to view your usage history. The easiest way to estimate them is to add the amounts you paid for the last 12 months and divide the total by 12.

If you are not separated and are still living in the marital home with your spouse, you can enter a proposed amount. Please specify whether you estimated or proposed these expenses.

Read through the subsections prior to completing them, as the financial affidavit may list some expenses under subsections you would not expect.

Household Expenses

- Monthly mortgage or rent
- Property taxes *only if your mortgage payment does not include them*
- Insurance on your home *only if your mortgage payment does not include it*
- Condo maintenance fees
- Homeowner's association fees
- Electricity
- Water, garbage and sewer
- Telephone (include cell phone if you have a landline and cell, or you can enter the cell phone expense on the "Other" lines)

- Fuel oil or natural gas

- Repairs and maintenance: Review the amounts you spent last year, add them and divide the amount by 12 to obtain an average

- Lawn care: Add the amounts and divide them by 12 unless your landscaper charges the same each month

- Pool maintenance: Add the amounts and divide them by 12 unless your monthly bill is the same each month

- Monthly pest control

- Monthly food and home supplies

- Meals outside the home

- Cable television

- Alarm service contract

- Service contracts on appliances

- Maid service

Total these expenses. You will need this number later.

Automobile Expenses

- Monthly gas and oil (if you include oil changes here, do not include them under 'Repairs')

- Monthly repairs

- Monthly tags and, if applicable, emissions testing

- Monthly vehicle insurance

- Monthly lease or financing payments

- Monthly rental or replacement

- Monthly public transportation or other alternative transportation, such as rideshare or carpool fees

- Monthly tolls and parking expenses

For amounts that vary, such as oil, gas, and repairs, add your expenses for the year and divide them by 12 to calculate an average monthly cost. Total this section. You will need this number later.

Monthly Expenses for Children Common to Both Parties

- Nursery, babysitting or daycare expenses
- School tuition
- School supplies, including books and fees not related to tuition
- After-school activities
- Lunch money
- Private lessons and tutoring
- Allowances
- Clothing and uniforms
- Entertainment for the children, such as movies and parties
- Child's health insurance expense
- Non-reimbursed medical, dental and prescriptions (do not include those covered by insurance)
- Psychiatric, psychological, and counseling expenses
- Orthodontic expenses
- Vitamins
- Beauty parlor or barbershop expenses
- Non-prescription medication (over-the-counter medications)
- Toiletries
- Gifts from your children to others
- Camp / summer activities
- Clubs, such as Boy Scouts or Girl Scouts
- Time-sharing expenses
- Miscellaneous expenses

Total this section, as you will need the total later.

Monthly Expenses for Children from Another Relationship

If you have expenses for children from a previous relationship, list those expenses in this section, but *do not* include child support payments.

Total the amount for this section. You will need this number later.

Monthly Insurance

If you have health insurance that you did not list under monthly household expenses or expenses for children common to both parties, you can list that here. Enter the subtotal, as you will need this number later.

If your child's premiums are included in your premiums, review your insurance policy for the breakdown.

Other Monthly Expenses Not Listed Above

- Dry cleaning
- Clothing expense
- Unreimbursed medical, dental and prescription expenses (do not include those covered by insurance or those expenses reimbursed by an employer or another party)
- Psychiatric, psychological and counseling expenses
- Non-prescription (over-the-counter) medications
- Grooming
- Gifts
- Pet expenses
- Club dues and memberships
- Sports and hobbies
- Entertainment
- Periodicals, books and music
- Vacations (average this over 12 months)
- Religious organizations
- Bank charges and credit card fees
- Education expenses
- Other usual and customary expenses not mentioned above

Total this section. You will need this number later.

Monthly Payments to Creditors

Using the last four digits of the account number and the creditor name, list the monthly amount paid to creditors. Do not include your mortgage or car payments.

Total this section.

Total Section II

Add the subtotals for all subsections of Section II. This amount is your total monthly expenses.

Summary

Subtract your total expenses from Section II from your total monthly net income from Section I. If the number is positive, this is the amount of surplus you have. Enter it on the appropriate line. If the number is negative, this is your monthly deficit. Enter it on the appropriate line.

Section III: Assets and Liabilities

Section A: Assets

Florida's family law affidavit provides an extensive table for assets. It features five columns divided into three sections.

Section A of the table contains an unmarked column and a place for you to list your assets. First, list the assets. Second, using the column to the left of the asset description, check the assets you wish the court to award you.

Section B of the table asks for the current fair market value. This is *not* what you paid for the item when it was brand new. It is what you can sell it for if you were to sell it today.

You can find the value of real estate on Zillow and other sites, but these are only estimates. The tax value on county property appraisers' websites is generally low.

Depending on your circumstances, you may have to obtain an appraisal for real property, especially if the other party does not agree with the value.

You can find the values of stocks, bonds, retirement plans and cash surrender values for life insurance on your account statements.

Section C of the table consists of two columns: "Petitioner" and "Respondent." If any item you list is nonmarital property, check the appropriate column for the party to whom it belongs. You can see an explanation of nonmarital or separate property under the Property Division chapter.

Ignore these two columns for all marital property. It only applies to separate property.

At the bottom of the table, total the assets.

Section B: Liabilities

This table is set up similarly to the Assets table in Section A. List liabilities, including mortgages, credit cards, bank loans, judgments, money owed to others and other monthly debts. In the column to the left, check the box if you want the court to award you that debt. This is common if the debt is in your name only and your spouse did not contribute to it. For example, a credit card solely in your name that your spouse has never used.

If the debt is joint or your spouse contributed to the debt, do not check this column.

If the debt is nonmarital—you or your spouse owned the debt prior to marriage or acquired the debt after the date of separation, check the appropriate column in Section C of the table.

In the 'Current Amount Owed' column, enter the current balance due. Total the column at the bottom of the table.

Section C: Net Worth

Figure your net worth by subtracting total liabilities from total assets. Enter that amount on the 'Total Net Worth' line. If the number is negative, be sure to place a minus sign before the number, or the court will read it as a positive number.

Section D: Contingent Assets and Liabilities

List any possible assets and liabilities in the two tables included in this section. A contingent asset includes income potential, accrued vacation or sick leave, bonuses, and inheritances that you have not yet received, among others.

A contingent liability is a possible lawsuit, future unpaid taxes, contingent tax liabilities and debts assumed by someone other than you.

Total both tables at the bottom of each.

Section E: Child Support Guidelines Worksheet

Check the appropriate box as to whether you will file a child support guidelines worksheet or not. If you have minor children, you must file the worksheet.

CHAPTER 30: MANDATORY DISCLOSURE

One of the first and most important steps of divorce is mandatory disclosure. Both parties exchange financial documents and information without waiting for a formal request (such as a request for production of documents) from the other side.

The goal is to ensure that both parties and the court have a clear and honest picture of the parties' financial situations. Mandatory disclosure includes financial affidavits, tax returns, pay stubs, and other relevant financial documents.

Rules governing mandatory disclosure are strict and include specific deadlines, usually within 30 to 45 days of the start of the case, depending on the state. The court can impose sanctions or unfavorable rulings if one or both parties fail to comply.

Gathering the required documentation before you file for divorce or as soon as your spouse serves you with a petition for divorce can significantly reduce stress throughout the divorce proceedings.

Once you have gathered all the documents applicable to your situation, organize them according to the mandatory disclosure statement. Make a copy for your attorney and a copy for your spouse's attorney—this could save you a significant amount of money if your lawyer does not have to do this.

The items required for mandatory disclosure include:

- The family law financial affidavit
- Federal and state personal income tax returns for the past three years
    - Include gift tax returns, foreign tax returns, and attachments to tax returns
    - Forms W-2, 1099, and K-1 for the **past year**
    - All schedules and worksheets
- Pay stubs for the past six months
    - Other evidence of earned income, such as income statements (sometimes referred to as profit and loss or P&L statements)
- A statement that identifies the source and amount of all income for the past six months for additional income not reflected on pay stubs.
- All forms of financial disclosure prepared for any purpose within the past 24 months, including:
    - Financial statements
    - Credit reports
    - Loan applications
- Real estate deeds, including property you no longer own, if you sold or transferred it in the past three years
- Promissory notes for the past 24 months
- Leases where you received rental income for the past three years
- Bank statements for the past 12 months, including:
    - Checking accounts
    - Savings accounts
    - Money market funds
    - Certificates of deposit
- Brokerage account statements for the past 12 months
    - Include accounts used for check-writing privileges
    - Copies of canceled checks and registers

- Retirement account statements for the past 12 months. Include:
  - Pension plans
  - Profit-sharing plans
  - Deferred compensation
  - Retirement plans, e.g., IRA, 401(k), 403(b), SEP, KEOGH accounts and other similar retirement plans.
- Virtual currency transactions and/or statements in which either party participated within the last 12 months, plus the most recent statement
- Life insurance policy declaration pages, last periodic statements and statements insuring you and/or your spouse for the past 12 months
- All health and dental insurance cards covering you, your spouse and dependent children
- Corporate, partnership, and trust tax returns for the past three years
- All credit card and charge account statements showing the parties' indebtedness as of the date of the filing of the divorce and the prior 24 months
- Promissory notes for the past 24 months, paid or unpaid
- Lease agreements you presently owe
- Premarital and marital agreements
- Declaration of non-paternity or judgments of disestablishment of paternity for any children born during the marriage
- Documents related to claims for an unequal distribution of marital property, enhancement or appreciation in nonmarital property and/or nonmarital status of an asset or debt
- Court orders directing that you pay or receive spousal support or child support

CHAPTER 31: FAMILY LAW INTERROGATORIES

If the other party serves you with interrogatories, you generally have a certain amount of time to answer them. Every state has its own timeframe, although a common timeframe is 30 days. We will use Florida's interrogatories as a sample. Depending on your state, yours may be different, but the document should have similar questions.

Interrogatories supplement the information you provided in mandatory disclosure and financial affidavits. Some information may overlap. This is an extensive document, and it is easy to feel overwhelmed when you first review it.

The best approach is to address one question at a time. Often, the document itself doesn't give you a lot of space to respond, especially if you are writing the answers by hand. Create a new document in your favorite word-processing program. Follow the numbering convention of the original document.

If you do not have access to a computer, you can do the same thing using lined notebook paper.

Section 1: Background Information

a. Your full legal name, any other names you go by

b. Present address (home address) and phone number

Section 2: Education

a. List all business, commercial and professional licenses. Include the license name, license number and the date you obtained it.

b. List all of our education. Include vocational training and specialized training.

- Name and address of educational institution #1

- Dates of attendance

- Degrees or certificates obtained (if you are currently attending, anticipated date of degree or certificate)

- Name and address of educational institution #2

- Dates of attendance

- Degrees or certificates obtained (if you are currently attending, anticipated date of degree or certificate)

- Name and address of educational institution #3

- Dates of attendance

- Degrees or certificates obtained (if you are currently attending, anticipated date of degree or certificate)

- Name and address of educational institution #4

- Dates of attendance

- Degrees or certificates obtained (if you are currently attending, anticipated date of degree or certificate)

Add the information for additional degrees or certificates as needed.

Section 3: Employment

For each place of employment or self-employment for the past three years:

- Name of employer
- Address and telephone number of your employer
- Dates of employment
- Job title
- Job description
- Starting salary
- Ending salary
- Name of direct supervisor
- List all benefits, including but not limited to:
    - Health, life and disability insurance
        - Name of insurance company
        - Policy number
    - Expense account
        - How much you spend per month
        - Items you expense, such as uniforms and dry cleaning.
    - Use of the company vehicle
        - Company business only, or allowed to use for personal business?
    - Vehicle expense reimbursement
        - How much per month
        - Items you expense, such as gas, maintenance, and insurance
    - Reimbursement for travel, food and lodging
        - Average monthly reimbursement
    - Dues for clubs or associations that your employer pays on your behalf
        - List club or association
        - List the amount per club or association
    - Pension or profit-sharing plans
        - Plan name
        - Amount contributed

- State the dates of any periods of unemployment during the past three years

Section 4: Assets

a. List all real estate you own or owned, including the marital home, during the past three years

- Street address or property #1
- Legal description of property (from the deed)
- Name and address of any other person or entity holding an interest
- Percentage of interest (e.g., one-half, one-third, etc.)
- Purchase price
- Cost of any improvements made since purchased
- Amount of depreciation taken (from tax returns)
- Fair market value on the date of separation
- Fair market value on the date of filing the petition for divorce

- Street address or property #2
- Legal description of property (from the deed)
- Name and address of any other person or entity holding an interest
- Percentage of interest (e.g., one-half, one-third, etc.)
- Purchase price
- Cost of any improvements made since purchased
- Amount of depreciation taken (from tax returns)
- Fair market value on the date of separation
- Fair market value on the date of filing the petition for divorce

- Street address or property #3
- Legal description of property (from the deed)
- Name and address of any other person or entity holding an interest
- Percentage of interest (e.g., one-half, one-third, etc.)

- Purchase price

- Cost of any improvements made since purchased

- Amount of depreciation taken (from tax returns)

- Fair market value on the date of separation

- Fair market value on the date of filing the petition for divorce

Add additional blocks of information if you own or owned more than three properties. Be sure to leave a space between them, as in the example above.

b. Tangible personal property you own or owned during the past three years, including but not limited to vehicles, tools, furniture, boats, jewelry, art objects, collections, and collectibles

- Name of property #1

- Percentage and type of interest you hold

- Names and address of person(s) holding any interest (e.g., car loan)

- Date you acquired the property/interest in the property

- Purchase price

- Present fair market value

- Fair market value on the date of separation

- Fair market value on the date of filing the petition for divorce

- Name of property #2

- Percentage and type of interest you hold

- Names and address of person(s) holding any interest (e.g., car loan)

- Date you acquired the property/interest in the property

- Purchase price

- Present fair market value

- Fair market value on the date of separation

- Fair market value on the date of filing the petition for divorce

- Name of property #3

- Percentage and type of interest you hold

- Names and address of person(s) holding any interest (e.g., car loan)

- Date you acquired the property/interest in the property

- Purchase price

- Present fair market value

- Fair market value on the date of separation

- Fair market value on the date of filing the petition for divorce

Add additional blocks of information for each piece of tangible personal property you own. Be sure to leave spaces between the blocks so they are easily identified.

 c. Intangible personal property. Do not include financial accounts listed elsewhere in this document. Otherwise, list all items of intangible personal property you own or owned in the past three years, including but not limited to partnership and business interests, goodwill, deferred compensation accounts unconnected with retirement, stock options, sick leave, vacation pay, stocks, bonds, stock funds, mutual funds, debts someone owes to you.

- Name of intangible personal property #1

- Percent of interest you hold

- Names and addresses of others holding any interest in the property, or the name and address of the person indebted to you

- Date you acquired your interest

- Purchase price, acquisition cost or loaned amount

- Fair market value or the amounts you claim are owned by or owed to you at the current time (the date you are completing these interrogatories

- Fair market value or the amounts you claim are owned by or owed to you on the date of separation from your spouse

- Fair market value or the amounts you claim are owned by or owed to you on the date of filing the petition for divorce

- Name of intangible personal property #2
- Percent of interest you hold
- Names and addresses of others holding any interest in the property, or the name and address of the person indebted to you
- Date you acquired your interest
- Purchase price, acquisition cost or loaned amount
- Fair market value or the amounts you claim are owned by or owed to you at the current time (the date you are completing these interrogatories
- Fair market value or the amounts you claim are owned by or owed to you on the date of separation from your spouse
- Fair market value or the amounts you claim are owned by or owed to you on the date of filing the petition for divorce

- Name of intangible personal property #3
- Percent of interest you hold
- Names and addresses of others holding any interest in the property, or the name and address of the person indebted to you
- Date you acquired your interest
- Purchase price, acquisition cost or loaned amount
- Fair market value or the amounts you claim are owned by or owed to you at the current time (the date you are completing these interrogatories
- Fair market value or the amounts you claim are owned by or owed to you on the date of separation from your spouse
- Fair market value or the amounts you claim are owned by or owed to you on the date of filing the petition for divorce

For each piece of intangible personal property, add another block of information, leaving spaces between each piece of property. Some states may allow you to produce periodic account statements as long as *all* of the information, including the date of acquisition, purchase price and current fair market value, is on the statement. Create a cover sheet for each piece of intangible personal property, stating its name, and place it as a divider between each type of property.

  d. Retirement accounts. For each of the following types of retirement accounts you have, list the required information. Accounts include:

- Defined benefit plans
    o Name and last four digits of the account number
    o Type of account plan
    o Name and address of the fiduciary plan administrator or service representative
    o Fair market value of your interest in the account/plan, including:
        ▪ Present value
        ▪ Value on the date of separation
        ▪ Value on the date of filing the petition for divorce
    o Vested or not? __ Yes __ No. If vested, in what amount_____ Date vested_____Schedule of future vesting:
    o Date you became or will become eligible to receive funds from this account
    o Monthly benefits of the account/plan, if not fair market value ascertained
    o Beneficiaries/alternate payees
- 401(k)
    o Name and last four digits of the account number
    o Type of account plan
    o Name and address of the fiduciary plan administrator or service representative
    o Fair market value of your interest in the account/plan, including:
        ▪ Present value
        ▪ Value on the date of separation
        ▪ Value on the date of filing the petition for divorce

- Name of intangible personal property #2
- Percent of interest you hold
- Names and addresses of others holding any interest in the property, or the name and address of the person indebted to you
- Date you acquired your interest
- Purchase price, acquisition cost or loaned amount
- Fair market value or the amounts you claim are owned by or owed to you at the current time (the date you are completing these interrogatories
- Fair market value or the amounts you claim are owned by or owed to you on the date of separation from your spouse
- Fair market value or the amounts you claim are owned by or owed to you on the date of filing the petition for divorce

- Name of intangible personal property #3
- Percent of interest you hold
- Names and addresses of others holding any interest in the property, or the name and address of the person indebted to you
- Date you acquired your interest
- Purchase price, acquisition cost or loaned amount
- Fair market value or the amounts you claim are owned by or owed to you at the current time (the date you are completing these interrogatories
- Fair market value or the amounts you claim are owned by or owed to you on the date of separation from your spouse
- Fair market value or the amounts you claim are owned by or owed to you on the date of filing the petition for divorce

For each piece of intangible personal property, add another block of information, leaving spaces between each piece of property. Some states may allow you to produce periodic account statements as long as *all* of the information, including the date of acquisition, purchase price and current fair market value, is on the statement. Create a cover sheet for each piece of intangible personal property, stating its name, and place it as a divider between each type of property.

d. Retirement accounts. For each of the following types of retirement accounts you have, list the required information. Accounts include:

- Defined benefit plans
  - Name and last four digits of the account number
  - Type of account plan
  - Name and address of the fiduciary plan administrator or service representative
  - Fair market value of your interest in the account/plan, including:
    - Present value
    - Value on the date of separation
    - Value on the date of filing the petition for divorce
  - Vested or not? __ Yes __ No. If vested, in what amount_____ Date vested_____Schedule of future vesting:
  - Date you became or will become eligible to receive funds from this account
  - Monthly benefits of the account/plan, if not fair market value ascertained
  - Beneficiaries/alternate payees
- 401(k)
  - Name and last four digits of the account number
  - Type of account plan
  - Name and address of the fiduciary plan administrator or service representative
  - Fair market value of your interest in the account/plan, including:
    - Present value
    - Value on the date of separation
    - Value on the date of filing the petition for divorce

- Vested or not? __ Yes __ No. If vested, in what amount_____
  Date vested_____ Schedule of future vesting:
- Date you became or will become eligible to receive funds from this account
- Monthly benefits of the account/plan, if not fair market value ascertained
- Beneficiaries/alternate payees

- 403(B)
  - Name and last four digits of the account number
  - Type of account plan
  - Name and address of the fiduciary plan administrator or service representative
  - Fair market value of your interest in the account/plan, including:
    - Present value
    - Value on the date of separation
    - Value on the date of filing the petition for divorce
  - Vested or not? __ Yes __ No. If vested, in what amount_____
    Date vested_____ Schedule of future vesting:
  - Date you became or will become eligible to receive funds from this account
  - Monthly benefits of the account/plan, if not fair market value ascertained
  - Beneficiaries/alternate payees
- IRA accounts
  - Name and last four digits of the account number
  - Type of account plan
  - Name and address of the fiduciary plan administrator or service representative
  - Fair market value of your interest in the account/plan, including:
    - Present value
    - Value on the date of separation

- ▪ Value on the date of filing the petition for divorce
  - o Vested or not? __ Yes __ No. If vested, in what amount_____ Date vested_____Schedule of future vesting:
  - o Date you became or will become eligible to receive funds from this account
  - o Monthly benefits of the account/plan, if not fair market value ascertained
  - o Beneficiaries/alternate payees
- Pension plans
  - o Name and last four digits of the account number
  - o Type of account plan
  - o Name and address of the fiduciary plan administrator or service representative
  - o Fair market value of your interest in the account/plan, including:
    - ▪ Present value
    - ▪ Value on the date of separation
    - ▪ Value on the date of filing the petition for divorce
  - o Vested or not? __ Yes __ No. If vested, in what amount_____ Date vested_____Schedule of future vesting:
  - o Date you became or will become eligible to receive funds from this account
  - o Monthly benefits of the account/plan, if not fair market value ascertained
  - o Beneficiaries/alternate payees
- Federal government plans
  - o Name and last four digits of the account number
  - o Type of account plan
  - o Name and address of the fiduciary plan administrator or service representative
  - o Fair market value of your interest in the account/plan, including:
    - ▪ Present value

- Value on the date of separation
- Value on the date of filing the petition for divorce
  - Vested or not? __ Yes __ No. If vested, in what amount_____ Date vested_____ Schedule of future vesting:
  - Date you became or will become eligible to receive funds from this account
  - Monthly benefits of the account/plan, if not fair market value ascertained
  - Beneficiaries/alternate payees
- State retirement accounts
  - Name and last four digits of the account number
  - Type of account plan
  - Name and address of the fiduciary plan administrator or service representative
  - Fair market value of your interest in the account/plan, including:
    - Present value
    - Value on the date of separation
    - Value on the date of filing the petition for divorce
  - Vested or not? __ Yes __ No. If vested, in what amount_____ Date vested_____ Schedule of future vesting:
  - Date you became or will become eligible to receive funds from this account
  - Monthly benefits of the account/plan, if not fair market value ascertained
  - Beneficiaries/alternate payees
- Money purchase plans
  - Name and last four digits of the account number
  - Type of account plan
  - Name and address of the fiduciary plan administrator or service representative
  - Fair market value of your interest in the account/plan, including:

- - Present value
  - Value on the date of separation
  - Value on the date of filing the petition for divorce
  - Vested or not? __ Yes __ No. If vested, in what amount_____ Date vested_____Schedule of future vesting:
  - Date you became or will become eligible to receive funds from this account
  - Monthly benefits of the account/plan, if not fair market value ascertained
  - Beneficiaries/alternate payees
- HR10 (Keogh) plans
  - Name and last four digits of the account number
  - Type of account plan
  - Name and address of the fiduciary plan administrator or service representative
  - Fair market value of your interest in the account/plan, including:
    - Present value
    - Value on the date of separation
    - Value on the date of filing the petition for divorce
  - Vested or not? __ Yes __ No. If vested, in what amount_____ Date vested_____Schedule of future vesting:
  - Date you became or will become eligible to receive funds from this account
  - Monthly benefits of the account/plan, if not fair market value ascertained
  - Beneficiaries/alternate payees
- Profit-sharing plans
  - Name and last four digits of the account number
  - Type of account plan
  - Name and address of the fiduciary plan administrator or service representative

- Fair market value of your interest in the account/plan, including:
  - Present value
  - Value on the date of separation
  - Value on the date of filing the petition for divorce
- Vested or not? __ Yes __ No. If vested, in what amount_____
  Date vested_____Schedule of future vesting:
- Date you became or will become eligible to receive funds from this account
- Monthly benefits of the account/plan, if not fair market value ascertained
- Beneficiaries/alternate payees
- Annuities
  - Name and last four digits of the account number
  - Type of account plan
  - Name and address of the fiduciary plan administrator or service representative
  - Fair market value of your interest in the account/plan, including:
    - Present value
    - Value on the date of separation
    - Value on the date of filing the petition for divorce
  - Vested or not? __ Yes __ No. If vested, in what amount_____
    Date vested_____Schedule of future vesting:
  - Date you became or will become eligible to receive funds from this account
  - Monthly benefits of the account/plan, if not fair market value ascertained
  - Beneficiaries/alternate payees
- Employee savings plans
  - Name and last four digits of the account number
  - Type of account plan

- o Name and address of the fiduciary plan administrator or service representative
- o Fair market value of your interest in the account/plan, including:
  - ▪ Present value
  - ▪ Value on the date of separation
  - ▪ Value on the date of filing the petition for divorce
- o Vested or not? __ Yes __ No. If vested, in what amount_____
  Date vested_____Schedule of future vesting:
- o Date you became or will become eligible to receive funds from this account
- o Monthly benefits of the account/plan, if not fair market value ascertained
- o Beneficiaries/alternate payees

e. Financial accounts, including checking, savings, money market, credit union accounts and other cash management accounts, whether held jointly with another person or your spouse or held solely. Add more blocks of data as needed to list all accounts.

- Name of the institution #1
- Address
- Name under which the account is or was maintained
- Last four digits of the account number
- Name of each person authorized to make withdrawals
- Highest balance within each of the preceding three years
  - o Year: _____ Balance: _____
  - o Year: _____ Balance: _____
  - o Year: _____ Balance: _____
- Lowest balance within each of the preceding three years
  - o Year: _____ Balance: _____
  - o Year: _____ Balance: _____
  - o Year: _____ Balance: _____

- Name of the institution #2
- Address
- Name under which the account is or was maintained
- Last four digits of the account number
- Name of each person authorized to make withdrawals
- Highest balance within each of the preceding three years
  - Year: _____ Balance: _____
  - Year: _____ Balance: _____
  - Year: _____ Balance: _____
- Lowest balance within each of the preceding three years
  - Year: _____ Balance: _____
  - Year: _____ Balance: _____
  - Year: _____ Balance: _____

- Name of the institution #3
- Address
- Name under which the account is or was maintained
- Last four digits of the account number
- Name of each person authorized to make withdrawals
- Highest balance within each of the preceding three years
  - Year: _____ Balance: _____
  - Year: _____ Balance: _____
  - Year: _____ Balance: _____
- Lowest balance within each of the preceding three years
  - Year: _____ Balance: _____
  - Year: _____ Balance: _____
  - Year: _____ Balance: _____

f. Closed financial accounts, including checking, savings, money market, credit union accounts and other cash management accounts, whether held jointly with another person or your spouse or held solely in the past three years (include accounts that you held an interest in another name). Add more blocks of data as needed for each closed account within the past three years.

- Name of the institution #1
- Name under which the account is or was maintained
- Last four digits of the account number
- Name of each person authorized to make withdrawals on the account
- Date account closed

- Name of the institution #2
- Name under which the account is or was maintained
- Last four digits of the account number
- Name of each person authorized to make withdrawals on the account
- Date account closed
-

g. Trusts. List any interest in an estate, trust insurance policy or annuity.

- If you are the beneficiary of any estate, trust, insurance policy or annuity, provide the following:
  - Name
  - Nature, amount and frequency of any distribution of benefits
  - Total value of the beneficiaries' interest in the benefits
  - Whether the benefit is vested or contingent
- If you have established a trust or you are the trustee of a trust, provide the following:
  - Date the trust was established
  - Names and addresses of the trustees
  - Names and addresses of the beneficiaries

    ○ Names and addresses of the persons or entities who possess the trust documents

    ○ Each asset that is held in each trust, with its fair market value

h. Cancelled insurance policies. List all policies canceled in the past three years, including policies you held, owned or had an interest in.

- Name of company #1
- Last four digits of account number
- Name and address of agent who issued the policy
- Amount of coverage
- Name of insured
- Name of owner of the policy
- Name of beneficiary #1
- Name of beneficiary #2
- Name of beneficiary #3
- Name of beneficiary #4
- Premium amount
- Date policy surrendered
- Amount, if any, of monies distributed to the owner

- Name of company #2
- Last four digits of account number
- Name and address of agent who issued the policy
- Amount of coverage
- Name of insured
- Name of owner of the policy
- Name of beneficiary #1
- Name of beneficiary #2
- Name of beneficiary #3
- Name of beneficiary #4

- Premium amount
- Date policy surrendered
- Amount, if any, of monies distributed to the owner

i. Name of accountant, bookkeeper or records keeper.

- Person or company who possessed financial records #1
- Address
- Phone number

- Person or company who possessed financial records #2
- Address
- Phone number

- Person or company who possessed financial records #3
- Address
- Phone number

j. Safe deposit boxes, lock boxes, vaults, etc. List the following for the past three years prior to filing the divorce petition:

- Name of bank, depository or other place you had a safe deposit box, lock box vault, etc. #1
- Were a signatory or co-signatory on a safe deposit box, lock box, vault, etc. #1
- Had access to a safe deposit box, lock box or vault #1
- Maintained property
- Box or identification number
- Name and address of each person who had access to any such depository during the same time period
- All persons who have possession of the keys or combination to the safe deposit box, lock box or vault
- Item #1 removed from the safe deposit box, lock box or vault

- o Fair market value
- Item #2 removed from the safe deposit box, lock box or vault
  - o Fair market value
- Item #3 removed from the safe deposit box, lock box or vault
  - o Fair market value
- Item #4 removed from the safe deposit box, lock box or vault
  - o Fair market value
- Item #1 currently in the safe deposit box, lock box or vault
  - o Fair market value
- Item #2 currently in the safe deposit box, lock box or vault
  - o Fair market value
- Item #3 currently in the safe deposit box, lock box or vault
  - o Fair market value
- Item #4 currently in the safe deposit box, lock box or vault
  - o Fair market value

- Name of bank, depository or other place you had a safe deposit box, lock box vault, etc. #2
- Were a signatory or co-signatory on a safe deposit box, lock box, vault, etc. #2
- Had access to a safe deposit box, lock box or vault #2
- Maintained property
- Box or identification number
- Name and address of each person who had access to any such depository during the same time period
- All persons who have possession of the keys or combination to the safe deposit box, lock box or vault
- Item #1 removed from the safe deposit box, lock box or vault
  - o Fair market value

- Item #2 removed from the safe deposit box, lock box or vault
  - Fair market value
- Item #3 removed from the safe deposit box, lock box or vault
  - Fair market value
- Item #4 removed from the safe deposit box, lock box or vault
  - Fair market value
- Item #1 currently in the safe deposit box, lock box or vault
  - Fair market value
- Item #2 currently in the safe deposit box, lock box or vault
  - Fair market value
- Item #3 currently in the safe deposit box, lock box or vault
  - Fair market value
- Item #4 currently in the safe deposit box, lock box or vault
  - Fair market value

- Name of bank, depository or other place you had a safe deposit box, lock box vault, etc. #3
- Were a signatory or co-signatory on a safe deposit box, lock box, vault, etc. #3
- Had access to a safe deposit box, lock box or vault #3
- Maintained property
- Box or identification number
- Name and address of each person who had access to any such depository during the same time period
- All persons who have possession of the keys or combination to the safe deposit box, lock box or vault
- Item #1 removed from the safe deposit box, lock box or vault
  - Fair market value
- Item #2 removed from the safe deposit box, lock box or vault

- o Fair market value
  - Item #3 removed from the safe deposit box, lock box or vault
    - o Fair market value
  - Item #4 removed from the safe deposit box, lock box or vault
    - o Fair market value
  - Item #1 currently in the safe deposit box, lock box or vault
    - o Fair market value
  - Item #2 currently in the safe deposit box, lock box or vault
    - o Fair market value
  - Item #3 currently in the safe deposit box, lock box or vault
    - o Fair market value
  - Item #4 currently in the safe deposit box, lock box or vault
    - o Fair market value

Section 5: Liabilities

a. Loans, liabilities, debts and other obligations other than credit cards and charge accounts. Add additional blocks of information as needed.

- Name of creditor #1
- Address of creditor
- Name(s) in which the obligation is or was incurred
- Last four digits of loan or account number
- Nature of security
- Payment schedule
- Present balance
- Current status of payments
- Total amount of arrearage, if any
- Balance on the date of separation
- Balance on the date of filing the petition for divorce

- Name of creditor #2
- Address of creditor
- Name(s) in which the obligation is or was incurred
- Last four digits of loan or account number
- Nature of security
- Payment schedule
- Present balance
- Current status of payments
- Total amount of arrearage, if any
- Balance on the date of separation
- Balance on the date of filing the petition for divorce

- Name of creditor #3
- Address of creditor
- Name(s) in which the obligation is or was incurred
- Last four digits of loan or account number
- Nature of security
- Payment schedule
- Present balance
- Current status of payments
- Total amount of arrearage, if any
- Balance on the date of separation
- Balance on the date of filing the petition for divorce

b. Credit cards and charge accounts. List all financial accounts in which you have or had any legal or equitable interest, whether in your name, jointly or in any other name. Create additional blocks of data as needed.

- Name of creditor #1
- Address of creditor
- Name under which the account was maintained

- Names of each person authorized to sign on the accounts

- Last four digits of the account number

- Present balance

- Current status of payments

- Total amount of arrearage, if any

- Balance on the date of separation

- Balance on the date of filing the petition for divorce

- Highest balance in

    o Year: _____ Highest balance: _____

    o Year: _____ Highest balance: _____

    o Year: _____ Highest balance: _____

- Lowest balance in

    o Year: _____ Highest balance: _____

    o Year: _____ Highest balance: _____

    o Year: _____ Highest balance: _____

- Name of creditor #2

- Address of creditor

- Name under which the account was maintained

- Names of each person authorized to sign on the accounts

- Last four digits of the account number

- Present balance

- Current status of payments

- Total amount of arrearage, if any

- Balance on the date of separation

- Balance on the date of filing the petition for divorce

- Highest balance in

    o Year: _____ Highest balance: _____

    o Year: _____ Highest balance: _____

- o Year: _____ Highest balance: _____
  - Lowest balance in
    - o Year: _____ Highest balance: _____
    - o Year: _____ Highest balance: _____
    - o Year: _____ Highest balance: _____

- Name of creditor #3
- Address of creditor
- Name under which the account was maintained
- Names of each person authorized to sign on the accounts
- Last four digits of the account number
- Present balance
- Current status of payments
- Total amount of arrearage, if any
- Balance on the date of separation
- Balance on the date of filing the petition for divorce
- Highest balance in
  - o Year: _____ Highest balance: _____
  - o Year: _____ Highest balance: _____
  - o Year: _____ Highest balance: _____
- Lowest balance in
  - o Year: _____ Highest balance: _____
  - o Year: _____ Highest balance: _____
  - o Year: _____ Highest balance: _____

c. Closed credit cards and charge accounts. For all credit cards, charge accounts, or other such accounts closed in the past three years, in which you have had a legal or equitable interest, regardless of whether the interest is or was held in your name individually or jointly or in any other name, list the following. Create additional blocks of data as needed.

- Name of creditor #1

- Address of creditor
- Name under which the account is or was maintained
- Last four digits of account number
- Name of each person authorized to sign on the account
- Date the balance was paid off
- Amount of the final balance paid off

- Name of creditor #2
- Address of creditor
- Name under which the account is or was maintained
- Last four digits of account number
- Name of each person authorized to sign on the account
- Date the balance was paid off
- Amount of the final balance paid off

- Name of creditor #3
- Address of creditor
- Name under which the account is or was maintained
- Last four digits of account number
- Name of each person authorized to sign on the account
- Date the balance was paid off
- Amount of the final balance paid off

Section 6: Miscellaneous

a. If you are claiming an unequal distribution of marital property or enhancement or appreciation of nonmarital property, state:
   - Property name/type #1
   - Amount claimed
   - Facts upon which you rely in your claim

- Property name/type #2
- Amount claimed
- Facts upon which you rely in your claim

- Property name/type #3
- Amount claimed
- Facts upon which you rely in your claim

b. If you are claiming that an asset or liability is nonmarital, list the asset or liability and all facts upon which you rely in your claim
- Asset or liability #1
- Facts

- Asset or liability #2
- Facts

- Asset or liability #3
- Facts

c. If the mental or physical condition of a spouse or child is an issue, identify the person and state the following:
- Name
- Health care provider #1
- Health care provider #2
- Health care provider #3

d. Detail your proposed parenting plan for the minor children, including your proposed time-sharing schedule. You can attach a copy of the completed parenting plan to answer this interrogatory.

e. If you are claiming the other parent's time-sharing with minor children should be limited, supervised or otherwise restricted, or that you should have sole parental responsibility for the minor children, with or without time-sharing with the other parent, or that you should have ultimate responsibility over specific aspects of the children's welfare or that the responsibilities should be divided between you and the other parent, state your reasons and all facts which you rely upon to support your claim.

Section 7: Long-form affidavit

If you filed the short-form affidavit, and you were specifically requested in the Notice of Service of Standard Family Law Interrogatories to file the long-form affidavit, you must do so within the time to serve the answers to these interrogatories.

Section 8: Signature Block

Complete the signature block. Some states may require you to notarize your answers.

APPENDIX 1: RESIDENCY REQUIREMENTS BY STATE

Alabama

One or both parties must have lived in Alabama for at least six months prior to filing the complaint for divorce. The petitioner must allege the residency of either party in the complaint. Furthermore, one of the parties must prove residency, usually by showing a driver's license or state identification card with an issue date at least six months prior to filing for divorce (Ala. Code §30-2-5).

Alaska

Neither party needs to allege residency to obtain a divorce in Alaska, although at least one spouse must be a resident of the state at the time of filing for divorce (Alaska Stat. §25.24.090).

Arizona

One of the parties must have lived in the state for at least 90 days prior to filing for divorce. The party may be domiciled in Arizona or can be a member of the Armed Forces and have had a military presence for at least 90 days (Ariz. Rev. Stat. §25-312).

Arkansas

To file for a divorce in Arkansas, at least one of the parties must be a resident for 60 or more days. Additionally, to obtain a divorce, one of the parties must be a resident of Arkansas for at least three months prior to the granting of the divorce decree. In the event of a default divorce, the petitioner must have been a resident of Arkansas for at least three months (Ark. Code Ann. § 9-12-307).

California

The residency requirements for California have two parts. At least one party must have been a resident of the state for six months prior to filing, plus a resident of the county where he or she is filing for divorce for at least three months.

Couples filing for same-sex divorce can file for divorce, even if they do not live in the state, as long as they were married in California and neither party lives in a jurisdiction that will dissolve the marriage. The county of marriage has jurisdiction over the divorce (Cal. Fam. Code §2320).

Colorado

At least one party to the divorce must be domiciled in Colorado for 91 days prior to filing for divorce or legal separation (Colo. Rev. Stat. §14-10-106).

Connecticut

At least one of the parties to the divorce must have lived in Connecticut for at least 12 months prior to filing for divorce. Exceptions include:

- A party who married while domiciled in the state returned to the state, intending to remain permanently or
- The cause for the divorce arose after either party moved to Connecticut or
- Any person who served or is currently serving in the Armed Forces or the Merchant Marines who was a resident of Connecticut at the time of entry, as the law considers that person to have continuously resided in the state.

(CT Gen Stat §46b-44. (Formerly Sec. 46-35). (2024).

Delaware

At least one party must have lived in or have been stationed in Delaware at least six months prior to filing a divorce or annulment action (Del. Code Ann. Tit. 13, §1504).

Florida

At least one party must be a resident of Florida for six months prior to filing a Petition for Dissolution of Marriage (Fla. Stat. §61.021).

Georgia

One party must have been a *bona fide* resident of Georgia for at least six months prior to filing a divorce petition. Members of the armed services must have resided in Georgia for one year prior to filing a divorce petition and can file in any county adjacent to a United States Army post or military reservation.

If the military member married a Georgia resident who has been living in Georgia for at least six months, the military member can file for divorce in the respondent's county of residence as long as the respondent has been a Georgia resident for at least six months (Ga. Code Ann. §19-5-2).

Hawaii

Either party must have been a resident of Hawaii for at least six months prior to filing for a divorce. Additionally, the party filing for divorce must have been a resident of the circuit where he or she is filing for divorce for at least three months prior to filing the divorce action (Haw. Rev. Stat. §580-1) (Hawaii State Judiciary: courts.state.hi.us/).

Idaho

At least one party must have resided in Idaho for at least six full weeks prior to filing for divorce (Idaho Code §32-701).

Illinois

At least one party must have been a resident of Illinois for at least 90 days prior to filing for divorce (750 Ill. Comp. Stat. 5/401).

Indiana

At least one party must have been a resident of Indiana for at least six months prior to filing for divorce. Additionally, at least one of the parties must have resided in the county of filing for at least three months prior to filing a divorce petition. The same rules apply to those stationed at a United States military installation in the state of Indiana.

If the court authorized a guardian for an incapacitated person, the guardian could file the petition for divorce on behalf of an incapacitated person in the guardian's county of residence as long as the guardian lived in that county for at least three months prior to filing the divorce petition (Ind. Code §31-15-2-6).

Iowa

One party must have been a resident of Iowa for at least one year prior to filing a divorce petition (Iowa Code §598.5).

Kansas

At least one party must have been a resident of Kansas for at least 60 days prior to filing for divorce. The same rule applies to those stationed at a United States Military Post or military reservation (Kan. Stat. Ann. §23-2703).

Kentucky

At least one of the parties must have been a resident of Kentucky for at least 180 days prior to filing a divorce action (Ky. Rev. Stat. Ann. §403.140).

Louisiana

At least one party must have resided in Louisiana for at least 180 days prior to filing a divorce action. However, if the parties have children, they must wait 365 days to file a divorce action in Louisiana (La. Civ. Code Ann. Art. 103).

Maine

At least one party must have lived in Maine for six or more months prior to filing a divorce action (Me. Rev. Stat. tit. 19-A, §901).

Maryland

One of the parties must have been a resident of Maryland for at least six months prior to filing a divorce action if the grounds for divorce happened outside of this state (Md. Code, Fam. Law §7-101).

Massachusetts

Either party can file for divorce in Massachusetts at any time, as long as the grounds occurred within the Commonwealth. However, if the grounds for divorce happened outside of the Commonwealth, the plaintiff must wait for one year to file for divorce (Mass. Gen. Laws ch. 208, §5).

Michigan

One of the parties must have lived in Michigan for at least 180 days prior to filing the divorce petition. Additionally, one of the parties must have lived in the county of filing for at least 10 days prior to filing.

Additionally, the 10-day county requirement does not apply if:

- The defendant was born in or is not a citizen of the United States,
- The parties have minor children, or
- Information exists that allows the court to reasonably believe that the defendant may abscond with the minor children to another country.

(Mich. Comp. Laws §552.9)

Minnesota

At least one party must have lived in or been domiciled in Minnesota for at least 180 days prior to filing a divorce action (Minn. Stat. §518.07).

Mississippi

At least one party must have been a resident of Mississippi for at least six months prior to filing an action for divorce (Miss. Code Ann. §93-5-5).

Missouri

One party must be a resident of Missouri for at least 90 days prior to filing for divorce or legal separation (Mo. Rev. Stat. §452.305).

Montana

One of the parties must be a resident of or domiciled in Montana for at least 90 days prior to filing a divorce action (Mont. Code Ann. §40-4-104).

Nebraska

At least one of the parties must have been a resident of Nebraska for one year prior to filing a divorce petition. The one exception to the rule is if the parties were legally married in Nebraska and lived in the state from the time of marriage (Neb. Rev. Stat. §42-349).

Nevada

One of the parties must have resided in Nevada for at least six weeks prior to filing an action for divorce (Nev. Rev. Stat. §125.020).

New Hampshire

The residency requirement for New Hampshire is at least one year prior to filing for divorce. Only one of the parties needs to meet this requirement (N.H. Rev. Stat. §458:5).

New Jersey

At least one party must be a resident of New Jersey for one year prior to filing for absolute divorce or from bed and board. The residency requirement also applies to the dissolution of civil unions or legal separations from partners in civil unions (N.J. Stat. Ann. §2A:34-10).

New Mexico

One party must have been a resident of New Mexico for at least six months prior to filing a divorce action (N.M. Stat. Ann. §40-4-5).

New York

The residency requirement for New York is one year if the parties:

- Were married or lived as a couple in the state,
- Lived in the state as husband and wife, and at least one of the parties has been a resident of New York for at least a year,
- The cause for the divorce occurred in New York, and either party had been a resident for at least one year prior to filing,
- The cause for divorce occurred in the state, and both parties are residents of the state.

If not, either party must have been a resident of New York for a continuous period of two years prior to filing for divorce (N.Y. Dom. Rel. Law §230).

North Carolina

At least one party must have been a resident of North Carolina for six months, or the parties must have separated at least one year prior to filing a divorce action (N.C. Gen. Stat. §50-8).

North Dakota

One of the parties must be a resident of North Dakota for at least six months prior to filing for divorce (N.D. Cent. Code §14-05-17).

Ohio

One of the parties must have been a resident of Ohio for at least six months prior to filing an action for divorce or an action for dissolution of marriage (Ohio Rev. Code §§3105.03, 3105.62).

Oklahoma

Either party must have lived in Oklahoma for at least six months prior to filing an action for divorce. The same rule applies to military members (Okla. Stat. tit. 43 §102).

Oregon

If a legal marriage occurred in Oregon and either party is a resident or is domiciled in the state, you do not have to meet a residency requirement. However, if the marriage did not occur in Oregon or when the petitioner alleges grounds, at least one party must meet the residency requirement of six months prior to filing for divorce.

In a legal separation suit, at least one of the parties must be a resident or domiciled in Oregon. (Or. Rev. Stat. §107.075).

Pennsylvania

One of the parties must have resided in the Commonwealth of Pennsylvania for at least six months prior to filing for divorce (23 Pa. Cons. Stat. §3104).

Rhode Island

At least one party to the divorce must have been a resident of Rhode Island for one year prior to filing the action (R.I. Gen. Laws §15-5-12).

South Carolina

If only one spouse is a resident of South Carolina, the parties must have resided in the state for one year prior to filing for divorce. However, if both parties are residents of the state, they must have resided in the state for three months prior to filing for divorce (S.C. Code Ann. §20-3-30).

South Dakota

The plaintiff in a divorce action must be a resident of South Dakota at the time of filing for divorce. Nonresident military members must be stationed in the state at the time of filing. The plaintiff does not need to maintain residency or military presence during the divorce proceedings (S.D. Codified Laws §25-4-30).

Tennessee

In most cases, at least one spouse must have lived in Tennessee for six months prior to filing the divorce action. However:

- If a case involves domestic violence, you do not have to meet the six-month residency requirement.
- Military spouses must reside in Tennessee for a year prior to filing a divorce action.

(Tenn. Code §36-4-105

Texas

One of the parties must have been domiciled in Texas for six months *and* must have resided in the county of filing for at least 90 days prior to filing a divorce action (Tex. Fam. Code §6.301).

Utah

At least one party to the divorce must have resided in Utah for at least 90 days prior to filing a divorce petition. The same rule applies to military members (Utah Code Ann. §30-3-1).

Vermont

One of the parties to the divorce must have resided in Vermont for at least six months prior to filing a divorce action and must have resided in the state for at least one year prior to the entry of the final judgment (15 V.S.A. §592).

Virginia

One of the parties must have been domiciled in Virginia for at least six months prior to filing an action for divorce. The same rule applies to military members, including those stationed on a ship with its home port in Virginia (Va. Code Ann. §20-97).

Washington

At least one party must claim Washington as his or her residence at the time of filing a petition for divorce. The same rule applies to military members (Wash. Rev. Code §26.09.030).

West Virginia

One of the parties must have been a resident of West Virginia for at least one year prior to filing a divorce action (W. Va. Code §48-5-103).

Wisconsin

One of the parties to a divorce must have been a *bona fide* resident of Wisconsin for at least six months and at least 30 days in the county of filing prior to filing for divorce (Wis. Stat. §767.301).

Wyoming

One of the parties must have resided in Wyoming for 60 days prior to filing a divorce action (Wyo. Stat. Ann. §20-2-107).

Appendix 11: Waiting Periods by State

Alabama

The court will not enter a final judgment of divorce until 30 days after the date of filing the summons and complaint. The court may enter temporary orders at any time during the proceedings (AL Code §30-2-8.1).

Alaska

The mandatory waiting period for divorce in Alaska was 30 days (Alaska R. Civ. P. 90.1)

Arizona

The court must wait 60 days after the date of service of process or the date of acceptance of process to enter a final judgment (Ariz. Rev. Stat. §25-329).

Arkansas

The mandatory waiting period for Arkansas is 30 days (Ark. Code Ann. §9-12-307(b)).

California

The court may not enter a final judgment of dissolution until six months have passed from the date of service of a copy of the summons and petition or the date of the respondent's appearance, whichever occurs first. The court may also extend the six-month waiting period "for good cause shown" (Cal. Fam. Code §2339(a), Cal. Fam. Code §2339(b)).

Colorado

The court may not enter a decree of dissolution of marriage or legal separation until 91 days after the court acquired jurisdiction over the respondent (Colo. Rev. Stat. §14-10-106(a)(III)).

Connecticut

The mandatory waiting period in Connecticut is 90 days following the second day after which a complaint for dissolution or legal separation is made returnable (CT Gen Stat §46b-67).

Delaware

The court may not rule on a petition for divorce for six months due to Delaware's separation laws (Del. Code Ann. Tit. 13, §1505(e)). For exceptions to the rule regarding marital misconduct, speak to an experienced family law attorney.

Florida

The court may not enter a final judgment of dissolution of marriage until 20 days have passed since the filing of the original petition for dissolution of marriage. However, if the parties can demonstrate an injustice by waiting 20 days, the court may enter the final judgment earlier (Fla. Stat. § 61.19).

Georgia

The court may not enter a final judgment until at least 30 days from the date of service on the respondent (Ga. Code Ann. §19-5-3(13).

Hawaii

The state of Hawaii does not have a waiting period; however, even an uncontested divorce can take 30 days or more.

Idaho

The court may not enter a final judgment until after you serve your spouse with divorce papers (Idaho Code §32-716).

Illinois

The state of Illinois no longer requires a 90-day waiting period for the court to enter a dissolution of marriage. It can enter the final judgment as soon as the parties complete the divorce proceedings, whether contested or uncontested (750 ILCS 5/401).

Indiana

The court may not enter a final judgment of dissolution of marriage until 60 days after the commencement of divorce proceedings (Ind. Code §31-15-2-10).

Iowa

The mandatory waiting period to obtain a final judgment of dissolution of marriage in Iowa is 90 days (Iowa Code §598.19).

Kansas

The mandatory waiting period to obtain a final judgment after you divorce is 60 days (Kan. Stat. Ann. 23-2708).

Kentucky

The courts in Kentucky cannot enter a final judgment until 60 days after the date of service of the summons (Ky. Rev. Stat. Ann. §403-044).

Louisiana

The court may not enter a judgment of divorce until 180 days after the service of the petition in divorces with no children and 365 days after the service of the petition when the couple has minor children (La. Civ. Code art. 103.1).

Maine

The state of Maine has no waiting period for obtaining a final judgment. It previously had a 60-day waiting period (Me. Rev. Stat. tit. 19-A §906).

Maryland

In 2023, Maryland changed its laws to drop the 12-month waiting period to six months. However, if the parties can agree on all factors and sign a marital settlement agreement, they do not have to endure a waiting period (Md. Code, Fam. Law §7-103).

Massachusetts

In Massachusetts, the court enters a judgment nisi, which does not take effect until 90 days after the court enters it (Mass. Gen. Laws ch. 208, §21).

Michigan

The waiting period in Michigan is 60 days from the time of filing the complaint or 180 days after filing the complaint if you have minor children under 18 years of age.

Minnesota

The statutes in Minnesota do not mandate a waiting period (Minn. Stat. §518.06).

Mississippi

The waiting period in Mississippi is 60 days (Miss. Code Ann. §93-5-2).

Missouri

The court must wait 30 days from the filing of the petition to enter a final judgment (Mo. Rev. Stat. §452.305).

Montana

You must live separate and apart for 180 days prior to filing a dissolution of marriage action in Montana. You can avoid the six-month separation if "there is serious marital discord which adversely affects the attitude of one of the parties (Mont. Code Ann. §40-4-104).

Nebraska

The court must wait 60 days after the perfection of service to enter a final judgment in a Nebraska divorce (Neb. Rev. Stat. § 42-361).

Nevada

You do not have to wait to obtain a divorce in Nevada; however, you must wait until your spouse responds to the petition. (Nev. Rev. Stat. §125.123, 125.120).

New Hampshire

You do not have to wait to obtain a divorce in New Hampshire; however, you must wait until your spouse responds to the petition (N.H. Rev. Stat. Ann. §458:7).

New Jersey

The court shall enter a final judgment after a hearing; therefore, New Jersey does not have a waiting period; however, you must wait until your spouse responds to the petition (N.J. Stat. Ann. § 2A:34-18).

New Mexico

You do not have to wait to obtain a divorce in New Mexico; however, you must wait until your spouse responds to the petition (N.M. Stat. Ann. §40-4-3).

New York

The State of New York does not have a mandatory waiting period for divorce (N.Y. Dom. Rel. Law § 170).

North Carolina

You must be separated and living in separate homes for one year and one day to obtain a divorce in North Carolina (N.C. Gen. Stat. §50-6).

North Dakota

The State of North Dakota does not have a mandatory waiting period for divorce (N.D. Cent. Code §14-05-09).

Ohio

The court may not enter a final judgment for at least 30 days after filing the action for divorce (Ohio Rev. Code Ann. §3105.64).

Oklahoma

You must wait at least 90 days from the date you file the divorce petition to obtain a final judgment in Oklahoma. However, if you do not have minor children, the waiting period is 10 days (Okla. Stat. tit. 12, R. 8).

Oregon

The state of Oregon does not have a mandatory waiting period for divorce.

Pennsylvania

You must wait for 90 days after the commencement of the divorce action to receive a final judgment (23 Pa. Cons. Stat. §3301(c)(1)).

Rhode Island

Once the court makes its decision, the final decree does not become operative until three months after the trial and decision. The court has 180 days after the initial three months to enter the final judgment. If 180 days have passed, the court can only enter the final decree in open court after one of the parties files a motion or with the written consent of the parties or their attorneys. Additionally, the parties may not remarry until the court enters the final decree (R.I. Gen. Laws §15-5-23).

South Carolina

The state of South Carolina requires the parties to separate for at least one year prior to the entry of the final judgment (S.C. Code Ann. §20-3-10(5)).

South Dakota

The court must wait for 60 days from the time the respondent was served with the complaint to enter a final judgment (S.D. Codified Laws §25-4-34).

Tennessee

The court cannot enter a final judgment until 60 days after the filing of the complaint if the parties do not have minor children and at least 90 days if the parties have minor children (Tenn. Code Ann. §36-4-101(b).

Texas

The court may not enter a final decree until 60 days after the date the petitioner files the petition for divorce. Texas has some exceptions to this rule, including:

- Annulments or a void marriage.
- The respondent has been convicted or received adjudication for an offense involving family violence.

- The petitioner has an active protective order or an active magistrate's order for emergency protection (Tex. Fam. Code §6.702, *et seq.*).

Utah

The waiting period in Utah is 90 days unless both parties complete the mandatory educational course for divorcing parents (Utah Code Ann. §30-3-18(1), (2).

Vermont

The state of Vermont enters a decree nisi at the end of a divorce trial. It does not become "absolute" until 90 days after the court enters it, thus creating a 90-day waiting period (15 V.S.A. §554).

Virginia

You must separate for six months if you have no minor children or one year if you have minor children before you can receive a divorce decree (Va. Code Ann. §20-91).

Washington

The courts in Washington cannot enter a divorce decree until 90 days after the petition was filed and the court issued the summons (Wash. Rev. Code § 26.09.030).

West Virginia

The court may not enter a final judgment in West Virginia until the respondent's 20 days to respond to the petition expire (Divorce Answer Packet Instructions WVSCA Form SCA-FC-100A; W. Va. Code §48-5-201).

Wisconsin

The court may enter a final judgment in a divorce proceeding 120 days after the service of the summons or 120 days after the parties file a joint petition (Wis. Stat. §767.335).

Wyoming

The court may not enter a final judgment in a divorce action until 20 days after the petitioner files the complaint (Wyo. Stat. Ann. §20-2-104).

APPENDIX III: RISK FACTORS FOR PSYCHOLOGICAL EVALUATIONS

When courts order psychological evaluations regarding custody, visitation and/or parental fitness, psychologists assess a range of risk factors to determine what arrangements serve the child's best interests while ensuring his or her safety and well-being. Risk factors may include:

Parenting Skills and Practices

The evaluator will assess whether a parent has the ability to provide for the child's basic needs, including food, shelter and medical care, maintain a safe environment and use age-appropriate, non-abusive discipline methods. Inadequate supervision or harsh discipline are red flags.

Additionally, the evaluator looks for consistency in routines and emotional responses that support a child's sense of security. Responsiveness to the child's emotional, physical and developmental needs is crucial for healthy attachment and development.

Mental Health Status

Poorly managed or untreated mental health conditions, such as depression, anxiety, bipolar and personality disorders, can impair parental capacity. Medical records for diagnoses, treatment history and current functioning can place a parent suffering from mental health issues in a better position if the parent is properly managing the condition.

The evaluator also looks for emotional instability, impulsive behavior and poor coping mechanisms, as these issues can jeopardize a child's safety and/or emotional well-being. The parent needs to have the ability to manage stress and regulate his or her emotions for effective parenting.

Substance Abuse

If a parent has current or past issues with drugs or alcohol, evaluators consider the severity, duration, treatment history, and, if in remission, the risk of relapse, as substance abuse can directly endanger children and/or impair parental judgment.

History or Allegations of Domestic Violence or Abuse

A parent who has any substantiated or credible allegations of abuse, whether directed at the child, the other parent, or others, can significantly impact custody and visitation decisions, as the court takes domestic violence and abuse very seriously. Evaluators may review police reports, court records and child protective services documentation.

Parental Fitness and Safety

When the evaluator examines the home environment, he or she looks for safety hazards, stability in housing and employment, and the presence of nurturing relationships.

Willingness to Co-Parent

Because it is almost always in the best interests of the child to have a loving and influential relationship with ***both*** parents, the court favors those who demonstrate a willingness and ability to work cooperatively with the other parent, including communicating effectively and prioritizing the child's needs over personal conflict.

Child's Mental Health and Developmental Needs

Evaluators assess the child's mental health, emotional adjustment and developmental milestones. Special needs and/or vulnerabilities may influence recommendations for custody or visitation.

Attachment and the Parent-Child Relationship

The strength and security of the child's attachment to each parent is a critical factor in determining custody and visitation. Evaluators look for healthy, positive relationships that support emotional development and resilience.

If the attachment is disputed or insecure, the evaluator may have cause for concern in his or her recommendations to the court.

Parental Alienation

If the evaluator finds evidence that one parent is attempting to alienate the child from the other, whether through manipulation, denigration or obstruction of contact, it can significantly influence custody decisions.

Exposure to Parental Conflict or Violence

When exposing a child to chronic high-conflict parental relationships or violence, you can harm a child's emotional and psychological well-being. Evaluators check for signs of distress, anxiety or behavioral problems linked to conflict within the family.

Criminal History

If a parent has any criminal convictions, especially those involving violence, substance abuse or crimes against children, the evaluator carefully reviews such documents for the potential impact that those issues may have on the child's safety and stability.

History with Child Protective Services

Any past or ongoing investigations or interventions by child protective services can indicate risk factors that the court needs to address or monitor. This could lead to supervised visitation and/or a forfeiture of legal custody.

The Parents' Childhood History

A parent's own history of trauma or adverse childhood experiences can influence his or her parenting style and capacity. Evaluators consider whether the parent has resolved these issues or if they pose ongoing risks.

Environmental and Social Factors

If the parents have the support of family, friends and community resources, it can buffer stress and enhance parenting. Conversely, isolation, poverty and/or unsafe neighborhoods can increase the risk and can influence the court's custody decisions.

ENDNOTES

[i] Patricia M. Hoff, *The Uniform Child-Custody Jurisdiction and Enforcement Act*, Office of Juvenile Justice and Delinquency Prevention, U.S. Department of Justice, December 2001, NCJ 189181, available at https://www.ojp.gov/pdffiles1/ojjdp/189181.pdf

[ii] Cornell Law School Legal Information Institute. "Pro Hac Vice." Accessed July 7, 2025. https://www.law.cornell.edu/wex/pro_hac_vice.

[iii] Office of Juvenile Justice and Delinquency Prevention. "The Uniform Child-Custody Jurisdiction and Enforcement Act." By Patricia M. Hoff. December 2001. Accessed July 7, 2025. https://www.ojp.gov/pdffiles1/ojjdp/189181.pdf.

[iv] Social Security Administration. "Eligibility for Family Benefits." Accessed June 9, 2025. https://www.ssa.gov/family/eligibility.

[v] U.S. Department of Defense. "Servicemembers Civil Relief Act (SCRA) Website." Accessed June 10, 2025. https://scra.dmdc.osd.mil/scra/#/home.

[vi] Defense Finance and Accounting Service. "Uniformed Services Former Spouses' Protection Act (USFSPA) – Legal Information." Accessed June 10, 2025. https://www.dfas.mil/Garnishment/usfspa/legal/.

[vii] U.S. Department of Justice. *Servicemembers Civil Relief Act*. Washington, DC: U.S. Department of Justice, 2011. https://www.justice.gov/sites/default/files/crt/legacy/2011/03/23/scratext.pdf.

[viii] 10 U.S.C. § 1408, "Payment of retired or retainer pay in compliance with court orders," accessed June 10, 2025, https://www.law.cornell.edu/uscode/text/10/1408.

[ix] Augusta Bar Association. "Military Divorce: The Uniformed Services Former Spouses' Protection Act (USFSPA)." Accessed June 10, 2025. https://augustabar.org/Resources/846.pdf.

[x] South Dakota Unified Judicial System. "Divorced Spouses of Military Service Members." Accessed June 10, 2025. https://ujs.sd.gov/self-help/get-legal-help/divorced-spouses-of-military-service-members/.

[xi] Internal Revenue Service. "Retirement Topics – QDRO – Qualified Domestic Relations Order." Accessed June 10, 2025. https://www.irs.gov/retirement-plans/plan-participant-employee/retirement-topics-qdro-qualified-domestic-relations-order

[xii] Nolo. "How Does Bankruptcy Affect a Pending Divorce Case?" Accessed June 11, 2025. https://www.nolo.com/legal-encyclopedia/if-i-file-bankruptcy-will-affect-pending-divorce-case.html.

[xiii] United States Courts. "Discharge in Bankruptcy – Bankruptcy Basics." Accessed June 11, 2025. https://www.uscourts.gov/court-programs/bankruptcy/bankruptcy-basics/discharge-bankruptcy-bankruptcy-basics.

[xiv] Custody X Change. "Birdnesting Divorce: Co-Parenting in the Same House." Accessed June 11, 2025. https://www.custodyxchange.com/topics/divorce/birdnesting.php.

[xv] Justia. "Grandparent Visitation & Custody Laws: 50-State Survey." Accessed June 13, 2025. https://www.justia.com/family/child-custody-and-support/grandparent-visitation-custody-laws-50-state-survey/

[xvi] Troxel v. Granville, 530 U.S. 57 (2000). Accessed June 13, 2025. https://supreme.justia.com/cases/federal/us/530/57/

[xvii] University of Tennessee Campbell County Agricultural Extension Service. "Co-Parenting | Campbell County - UT Extension." Accessed June 13, 2025. https://campbell.tennessee.edu/co-parenting/

[xviii] Kids First. "Kids First Program – Hawai'i State Judiciary." Accessed June 13, 2025. https://kidsfirsthawaii.com/.

[xix] Hawaii State Legislature. "Senate Bill 1159, 2008 Regular Session." Accessed June 13, 2025. https://data.capitol.hawaii.gov/sessions/session2008/bills/SB1159_.htm.

[xx] Third Judicial District of Idaho. "Focus on Children." Accessed June 13, 2025. https://www.thirdjudicialcourt.idaho.gov/fcs/focus-on-children/.

[xxi] Massachusetts Probate and Family Court. "Probate and Family Court Standing Order 3-23: Co-parenting education course for married and unmarried parents." Accessed June 13, 2025. https://www.mass.gov/probate-and-family-court-rules/probate-and-family-court-standing-order-3-23-co-parenting-education-course-for-married-and-unmarried-parents.

[xxii] Michigan Judicial Branch. "SMILE Program." Accessed June 13, 2025. https://micase.state.mi.us/micaseapp/public/smile.html

[xxiii] Psychology Today. "Parental Alienation." Accessed June 13, 2025. https://www.psychologytoday.com/us/basics/parental-alienation.

[xxiv] LawInfo. "Child Witnesses in Family Law Cases." Accessed June 13, 2025. https://www.lawinfo.com/resources/family-law/child-witnesses-in-family-law-cases.html.

[xxv] TexasLawHelp.org. "Child Support and Lower Incomes." Accessed June 13, 2025. https://texaslawhelp.org/article/child-support-and-lower-incomes#:~:text=1%20child%20=%2015%25%20of%20the,support%20ends%20for%20each%20child.

[xxvi] Mississippi Department of Human Services. *Mississippi Child Support Guidelines*. Revised May 2020. Accessed June 13, 2025. https://www.mdhs.ms.gov/wp-content/uploads/2020/05/Child-Support-Guidelines-Revised.pdf.

[xxvii] North Dakota Department of Health and Human Services. *Final Amended Child Support Guidelines, July 2023*. Accessed June 13, 2025. https://www.hhs.nd.gov/sites/www/files/documents/child-support/final-amended-guidelines-july-2023.pdf.

[xxviii] Alaska Court System. *How to Calculate Child Support Under Civil Rule 90.3 (DR-310)*. September 2023. Accessed June 13, 2025. https://public.courts.alaska.gov/web/forms/docs/dr-310.pdf.

[xxix] Mississippi Department of Human Services. *Mississippi Child Support Guidelines*. Revised May 2020. Accessed June 13, 2025. https://www.mdhs.ms.gov/wp-content/uploads/2020/05/Child-Support-Guidelines-Revised.pdf

^{xxx} Wisconsin Department of Children and Families. "Estimating Child Support Amounts." Accessed June 13, 2025. https://dcf.wisconsin.gov/cs/order/tools.

^{xxxi} Wisconsin Department of Children and Families. *High-Income Payer Worksheet to Estimate Support under DCF 150*. June 2024. Accessed June 13, 2025. https://dcf.wisconsin.gov/files/cs/order/worksheet-high-income.pdf.

^{xxxii} Wisconsin Department of Children and Families. *Chapter DCF 150 Appendix C: Child Support Obligation of Low-Income Payers at 75% to 150% of the 2024 Federal Poverty Guidelines*. Effective March 1, 2024. Accessed June 13, 2025. https://docs.legis.wisconsin.gov/code/admin_code/dcf/101_199/150_c.

^{xxxiii} North Dakota Department of Health and Human Services. "Final Amended Child Support Guidelines, July 2023." Accessed June 14, 2025. https://www.hhs.nd.gov/sites/www/files/documents/child-support/final-amended-guidelines-july-2023.pdf

^{xxxiv} North Dakota Department of Health and Human Services. "Guidelines Schedule with Percentages." Revised October 1, 2021. Accessed June 14, 2025. https://www.hhs.nd.gov/sites/www/files/documents/child-support/guidelines-schedule-with-percentages.pdf

^{xxxv} Texas Family Code § 154.001 et seq. "Child Support." Texas Statutes. Accessed June 14, 2025. https://statutes.capitol.texas.gov/Docs/FA/htm/FA.154.htm.

^{xxxvi} Nevada Department of Health and Human Services. "Nevada Child Support Guidelines." Revised July 1, 2023. Accessed June 14, 2025. https://dwss.nv.gov/uploadedFiles/dwssnvgov/content/Support/cs_MASTER_DOCUMENT_final.pdf

^{xxxvii} SupportPay. "The Melson Formula – Child Support." Accessed June 14, 2025. https://supportpay.com/the-melson-formula-child-support/

^{xxxviii} Family Court of the State of Delaware. "2025 Delaware Child Support Formula (Form 509, Rev. 2/25 V2.01)." Accessed June 14, 2025. https://courts.delaware.gov/forms/download.aspx?id=268

^{xxxix} Family Court of the State of Hawaiʻi. "Child Support Guidelines Worksheet." Revised December 30, 2014. Accessed June 14, 2025. https://www.courts.state.hi.us/docs/form/oahu/child_support/csg_a_child_support_worksheet.pdf

^{xl} Montana Department of Public Health and Human Services. "Montana Child Support Guidelines: Worksheets." Accessed June 14, 2025. https://www.dshs.wa.gov/sites/default/files/ESA/dcs/documents/15Montana%20Worksheets.pdf

^{xli} "Adoption Home Study Requirements by State." Adoption Network. Accessed July 8, 2025. https://adoptionnetwork.com/adoption-laws-by-state/homestudy-requirements/

^{xlii} Justia. "Modifying Child Custody or Support." Accessed June 14, 2025. https://www.justia.com/family/child-custody-and-support/modifying-child-custody-or-support/

^{xliii} "Uniform Premarital Agreement Act." Cornell Law School Legal Information Institute. Accessed July 8, 2025. https://www.law.cornell.edu/wex/uniform_premarital_agreement_act

^{xliv} "Florida Statutes § 61.079: Premarital agreements." The Florida Legislature. Accessed July 8, 2025. http://www.leg.state.fl.us/Statutes/index.cfm?App_mode=Display_Statute&URL=0000-0099/0061/Sections/0061.079.html

GLOSSARY

Abandonment

When one person leaves another, like a spouse or child, without planning to return or provide support. State laws often dictate the amount of time a spouse has to be gone without the intention of returning.

Adoption

The legal process of becoming the parent of a child who is not your biological child.

Affidavit

A written statement that someone swears is true, usually signed in front of a notary.

Alimony (Spousal Support)

Money that one spouse may have to pay the other after a divorce to help support the other for a period of time.

Appeal

Asking a higher court to review or change a decision made by a lower court.

Asset

Anything valuable that a person owns, like money, a house, or a car.

Beneficiary

A person who receives money or property from a will, insurance policy, or trust. You can also list beneficiaries on bank accounts and certain other types of financial accounts.

Child Custody

A court's decision about which parent a child will live with and who will make important decisions for the child. The parents can also make this decision on their own during settlement negotiations.

Child Support

Money that a parent pays to help cover the costs of raising their child after separation or divorce.

Community Property

Property and money earned by a married couple that is owned equally by both.

Contempt of Court

Not following a court order, which can lead to penalties.

Contested Divorce

A divorce where the two people do not agree on one or more important issues, like money or child custody.

Custodial Parent

The parent a child lives with most of the time.

Debt (Liability)

Money that someone owes to another person or company.

Default Divorce

A divorce that happens because one spouse does not respond to court papers or show up in court.

Deposition

A meeting where someone answers questions under oath before a trial.

Discovery

The process where both sides in a legal case share information and documents with each other.

Dissolution of Marriage

Another term for divorce; the legal end of a marriage.

Domestic Violence

Abuse or violence between people in a family or household.

Equitable Distribution

A way to divide property fairly, but not always equally, between divorcing spouses.

Guardian *ad Litem* (GAL)

A person the court chooses to represent the best interests of a child in a legal case.

Hearing

A meeting in court where a judge listens to both sides before making a decision.

Income Shares Model

A way to figure out child support based on the income of both parents.

Injunction (Restraining Order)

A court order that tells someone to stop doing something, like contacting another person.

Joint Custody

Both parents share the responsibility of caring for and making decisions about their child.

Jurisdiction

The power or authority a court has to make decisions in a case.

Legal Custody

The right and responsibility to make important decisions about a child's life, such as education, healthcare, and religion. The court can give legal custody to one parent (sole legal custody) or both parents (joint legal custody).

Legal Separation

A court order that allows married people to live apart but stay legally married.

Liability

Another word for debt; something a person owes.

Mediation

A process where a neutral person helps people solve their disagreements without going to court.

Modification

A change to a court order, like changing child support or custody.

No-Fault Divorce

A divorce where neither person has to prove the other did something wrong.

Non-Custodial Parent

The parent with whom a child does not live most of the time.

Parenting Plan

A written agreement about how parents will take care of their child after separation or divorce.

Petition

A written request asking the court to do something, like start a divorce.

Physical Custody

Refers to where a child lives and who takes care of the child's daily needs. Physical custody can be with one parent (sole physical custody) or shared between both parents (joint physical custody).

Plaintiff (Petitioner)

The person who starts a legal case.

Postnuptial Agreement (Postnup)

A legal contract made between spouses after they are married. It explains how the spouses will divide money, property, and debts if the couple divorces or one spouse dies. A postnuptial agreement can help clarify financial responsibilities, protect certain assets, or update earlier agreements. Both spouses must agree to it freely, and it must be in writing to be valid.

Prenuptial Agreement (Prenup)

A contract made before marriage about how the couple will divide property and money if the couple divorces.

Pro Se

Representing yourself in court without a lawyer.

Property Division

How people split money, property, and debts when they divorce.

Respondent (Defendant)

The person who responds to a legal case started by someone else.

Restraining Order

A court order to protect someone from being harmed or contacted by another person.

Settlement

An agreement between both sides in a legal case, usually before going to trial.

Spousal Support (Alimony)

See "Alimony" above.

Subpoena

A court order that makes someone go to court or provide documents.

Testimony

What a person says under oath in court.

Uncontested Divorce

A divorce where both people agree on all the important issues.

Visitation (Parenting Time)

The time a non-custodial parent spends with his or her child.

INDEX

Q

R

S

ABOUT THE AUTHOR

Cheryl Bowman received an A.S. in Legal Studies in 1996 and freelanced until she started working in a law office in 2003. Her work encompasses most areas of civil law and some criminal law, but she prefers family law and bankruptcy. She worked for two law offices from 2003 until 2008. In 2007, she started freelancing legal articles, making that her full-time work.

In 2009, the first law office she worked for disbanded and the senior partner, who became a sole practitioner, asked her to freelance for him. She freelanced for him until his death in 2016, while still writing legal articles, which she still does to this day.

Some of Cheryl's accomplishments include working on the draft of the initial appeal brief that went to the state's Supreme Court and changed how Hillsborough County, Florida, treats passive income and high-asset bankruptcy cases.